The Teacher's

IDEA BOOK

THE HIGH/SCOPE PRESS
A division of the
High/Scope Educational Research Foundation
600 N. River St.
Ypsilanti, Michigan 48198

Daily Planning Around the Key Experiences

Michelle Graves

THE HIGH/SCOPE PRESS
Ypsilanti, Michigan

THE HIGH/SCOPE PRESS
A division of the
High/Scope Educational Research Foundation
600 N. River St.
Ypsilanti, Michigan 48198

Photography by Gregory Fox, Ann Arbor
Cover and text design by Linda Eckel, Ypsilanti

Library of Congress Cataloging in Publication Data: LC 88-35794

ISBN 0-931114-80-2

Printed in the United States of America

Contents

Preface

When educators are asked, "What do you hope children will gain from your educational program?" they will often respond with answers like these:

"We want them to learn to think on their own, to be independent."

"We want them to gain a love of learning and to have a chance to be creative."

"We want them to learn at their own rates."

"We want them to develop a sense of responsibility and self-reliance."

All of these responses reflect the intuitive belief of many educators that early childhood programs should help children become **self-reliant problem-solvers** who can set their own goals and follow through on them independently. In the High/Scope Curriculum, we work toward this goal by offering children opportunities, within a carefully planned daily routine, to work and play independently, to make choices, to pursue their own interests, and to solve the problems that arise during this process. The focus throughout the school day is on children's own choices and decisions, guided and supported by adults who are aware of the children's developmental needs. We offer this book as one tool that teachers and caregivers can use in creating classroom or day care environments that encourage children to chart their own courses.

Research on Curriculum Effects

Our belief in child-initiated learning has been reaffirmed continually in years of work with young children and the adults who teach and care for them. In recent years research findings from High/Scope's long-term studies have begun to confirm the lessons of our experience.* These studies suggest that preschool programs that encourage children's

*For Curriculum Comparison Project findings, see L. J. Schweinhart, D. P. Weikart, and M. B. Larner, "Consequences of Three Preschool Curriculum Models Through Age 15," *Early Childhood Research Quarterly,* Vol. 1, No. 1 (1986), pp.15 – 35 (reprint available from High/Scope Press, Ypsilanti, MI). For Perry Preschool Program findings, see L. J. Schweinhart et al., *Changed Lives: The Effects of the Perry Preschool Program on Youths Through Age 19,* Monographs of the High/Scope Educational Research Foundation, 8 (Ypsilanti, MI: High/Scope Press, 1984).

self-directed learning do indeed have a positive impact on children's later lives.

One such High/Scope research effort, our Curriculum Comparison Project, has been following three groups of children who experienced three very different preschool programs in the late 1960s. One group of children in the study attended a High/Scope Curriculum preschool program; the second, a program based on traditional nursery school methods; and the third, a highly structured program in which most of the activities were teacher-directed. In the first two programs, children were frequently encouraged to choose their own activities, in contrast to the strong emphasis on direct instruction in the third program.

The findings from the three groups are intriguing. While children who attended all three programs made substantial intellectual gains, recent findings indicate important differences in social behavior among the three groups. For example, it appears that children from the programs that emphasized self-initiated learning had a much lower risk of delinquent behavior in later years than children who attended the direct-instruction program.

Another High/Scope study suggesting a link between preschool experiences and important areas of adult life success is the Perry Preschool Study. This High/Scope study has been following into adulthood the disadvantaged children who attended the Ypsilanti Perry Preschool in the early 1960s. The classroom program used was an early version of the High/Scope Curriculum, and the program also included regular home visits. Long-term findings indicate that children who had the preschool program performed better in grade school and junior high, were less likely to be placed in special education, and were less likely to repeat a grade in later schooling than children in a comparable group who had no preschool. In later years, the group of children who had preschool also had lower rates of delinquency, teen pregnancy, welfare use, and illiteracy; were less likely to be school dropouts; and had higher rates of employment and enrollment in college and technical schools.

To us, findings from both these studies strengthen our common-sense belief that encouraging preschool children to make choices and follow through on them may lead them to a deeper sense of social responsibility and to greater academic and economic success in adult life. This book is intended to guide teachers in providing such learning activities that grow from children's personal choices and interests.

History of the Curriculum

The educational approach used in this book, the High/Scope Curriculum (formerly known as the Cognitively Oriented Curriculum), has been under development since the 1960s and now reflects the contributions of numerous educators. David P. Weikart and his colleagues began developing the curriculum in 1961, when Weikart was special education director for the Ypsilanti, Michigan, Public Schools. In 1970, Weikart founded the High/Scope Educational Research Foundation to continue curriculum development activities and to conduct related research studies.

Jean Piaget's theories of child development have been a major influence in the evolution of the High/Scope approach. The curriculum is structured to support children's development in key areas identified in Piaget's theories. In each of these key areas, the curriculum identifies "key experiences," fundamental activities and processes through which children can develop important skills and learn basic concepts. This book is organized around these key experiences.

Piagetian theory is not the only influence that has shaped our curriculum; much has also been adapted from the work of other educators and from traditional nursery school practice. Our approach continues to evolve and change. Recently, we have been integrating materials and methods developed by other educators in specific skill areas. For example, we have been exploring the applications of some of the better educational computer programs to our early childhood approach. We are also rethinking our key experiences to include a more explicit emphasis on social and emotional development and to incorporate aspects of Phyllis Weikart's music and movement curriculum. Future editions of this book will incorporate the results of these ongoing development efforts.

How This Book Was Conceived

This book is a direct outgrowth of a training project in which I worked with preschool educators from southeastern Michigan who were responsible for training others to use the High/Scope Curriculum. During the last of our seven weeks together, a subset of the group took on the task of recording the ways in which the High/Scope key experiences could be encouraged during different parts of the daily routine. As I took their chart pads filled with ideas back to my office, I thought about my own classroom experiences and was inspired to add more ideas to their lists. Gradually, what started as a two-day activity evolved into a two-year project that became this book. Over the course of this project, I've very much appreciated the inspiration and ideas of the educators who participated in that original project: Pamela Clark, Barbara Crandall, Constance Debbaudt, Kathleen Fink, Sandy Ford, Kim Grossman, Pat Hagen, Phyllis Hodge, Patricia Howard, Denise Kluck, Barbara Knibbs, Patricia MacFadyn, Elizabeth Martin, Barbara Papania, Maryellen Passerman, Diane Sharples, Debra Spring-Ross, Heidi Thornley, Becki Zehnder, and Gayle Zimmerer. I'm also grateful to the teaching staff in the many classrooms I've had the opportunity to visit during my involvement in this and other training projects.

In addition, I would like to thank David Weikart for his vision of developmentally appropriate education and for the opportunity afforded to me to put this vision into practice through the development of this book. I am also indebted to Mary Hohmann and Bernard Banet, who, along with David Weikart, wrote the High/Scope preschool manual *Young Children in Action*. This comprehensive guide has greatly influenced my work with children by clarifying both the philosophical underpinnings of the High/Scope approach and its practical applications. Special thanks are extended to Mary Hohmann for reviewing the manuscript of this book. Her extensive suggestions for rewording and expanding the teaching strategies in terms of High/Scope's key experiences resulted in many improvements. I would also like to acknowledge the contributions of Warren Buckleitner and Charles Hohmann, whose suggestions for computer learning activities are incorporated throughout the text.

Finally, I want to thank my editor, Nancy Altman Brickman, for her continued support in pursuing this project. She has been responsible for forming all the pieces of this project into a cohesive whole. Her comments about the content as they related to her own preschool-aged children reassured me that this book could be useful in helping people define "developmentally appropriate" in everyday terms.

Michelle Graves

INTRODUCTION

In the past 12 years I have had extensive experience with the High/Scope Curriculum, first as a classroom teacher and later as a trainer of other early childhood teachers and administrators. Over the years, I have become familiar with the rewards and challenges of creating developmentally appropriate learning environments.

Both in my own teaching and in training other teachers, I have found that defining "developmentally appropriate" in practical terms is a very difficult process. Though the philosophy of developmentally appropriate education is appealing to many educators, they often find themselves at a loss when they attempt to apply it in their day-to-day work with children. After all, most educators were themselves educated in traditional settings, shaped by the need for children to learn "right answers." When teaching adults are released from the burden of transmitting right answers, their role becomes more difficult to define. For these educators, who have given up the drills, workbooks, and other mainstays of traditional education, the question is often "What now?"

During my struggle to come up with a working definition of developmentally appropriate education, I recorded my own language when working with children, and I listened to many others describe their teaching and training experiences. I continually asked educators and caregivers for feedback on the difficulties they encountered in using a curriculum that stresses child-initiated learning. Here is a sampling of their concerns:

> *"After being briefed about High/Scope's approach, my main question is how important concepts will be practiced without the use of seat work and teacher-directed activities."*

> *"If the children do not decide in their plans to work with numbers, colors, and shapes, what should I do?"*

> *"I'd like to try out the ideas [from the workshop] for giving my children choices in their art work. But every time I do, the parents question me about why their children don't come home with cute art projects like their brothers and sisters used to when they were in preschool."*

The common thread in these comments is a concern that when children are encouraged to choose their own learning experiences, they will no longer learn the concepts and facts that most people see as the indicators of educational success. If teachers don't teach such concepts directly, how and what will young children learn?

Another theme that runs through the comments I've heard from teachers, caregivers, and teacher-trainers, is that once teachers are given suggestions for replacing the patterns, dittos, flashcards, and worksheets that are used in many school settings, they are satisfied with the results of their new learning environments both for themselves and for the children. For example:

> *"After last month's workshop on number I realized that I was not doing enough in this area. So now I am trying to use some of the strategies that were presented, such as counting objects on a collage and writing the number."*

> *"One situation that pleased me happened in the block center. Kaman and Phat were using some newly added colored blocks to make spaceships on the rug. Phat was building a model of the space shuttle and together we drew a picture of it. Phat talked about the color names and block shapes as he was drawing."*

So then . . . How and what should children learn? What should the classroom look like? What should adults do and say at planning time, work time, recall time, small-group time, and circle time? This book is designed to answer such concrete questions. We've tried to make it a handy sourcebook that teachers and caregivers can consult whenever they need specific suggestions and strategies for encouraging developmentally appropriate learning experiences.

I hope the book will be helpful to you in the following ways:

☐ In suggesting developmentally appropriate materials you can use for stocking your classroom work areas

☐ In helping you think about the language you can use to encourage children to express and build upon their own ideas

☐ In pointing out how to teach important concepts without direct instruction

☐ In helping you define the components that make up a consistent daily routine that accommodates children's individual needs and encourages their creativity

The book is designed so that you can select those strategies and suggestions that seem most appropriate to your program. Our hope is that as you put these ideas into practice, your children will inspire you to think of additional ways to extend and work with the key concepts.

Overview of This Booklet

The section that follows provides a brief overview of the High/Scope Curriculum that sets the rest of the book in context. The curriculum's philosophy, daily routine, guidelines for room arrangement, and key experiences are reviewed. Following this we describe our approach

to team teaching and planning and provide guidelines for using this book to plan in a team around the key experiences and the children's interests.

Following this introductory material is the heart of the book: chapters providing specific teaching suggestions for each group of key experiences. **Key experiences** is the term we use to describe *general kinds of activities that exercise important abilities developing in preschoolers.* In each chapter, we provide a brief overview of the fundamental skills, processes, and concepts covered by that set of key experiences, followed by specific strategies for focusing on them during each segment of the daily routine. Suggestions are given for planning time, work time, recall time, small-group time, and circle time.

The lists of strategies for teaching are not parallel in format: some of them are suggestions for group activities, some are general teaching strategies that can be applied to any activity, some are ideas for materials or room arrangement, some are simply words or phrases a teacher can use to focus a moment's attention on a particular concept. We have made no attempt to organize our teaching suggestions into structured sequences because they are not intended to be used as explicit lesson plans. Ours is an **open framework curriculum.** Instead of prescribed sequences of classroom activities, we offer a set of principles and practices that can guide teachers and caregivers in developing their own programs. We believe the actual day-to-day curriculum should be planned around the interests, needs, and styles of the particular group of children involved and the adults who work with them.

This book is designed to be most useful to educators who have received or are receiving training in implementing the High/Scope Curriculum. *Please note that it does not contain a comprehensive description of our curriculum approach.* For more complete information on the High/Scope Curriculum and the developmental theory behind it, we suggest you consult the High/Scope preschool manual, *Young Children in Action,* or attend a High/Scope training workshop.

Overview of the High/Scope Approach

A guiding principle of the High/Scope Curriculum is the belief that *young children are capable of making decisions and solving problems* about activities that are interesting to them personally. Teachers and caregivers then use these personal interests as the springboard for teaching the social and academic concepts needed to be successful in this society.

Another key element of the High/Scope approach is **developmental validity:** We believe that children develop in predictable sequences, that there are optimal times for particular kinds of learning, and that there are teaching methods that are more appropriate at certain times in the developmental sequence than at others.

Active Learning

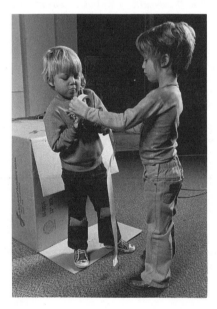

Based upon our knowledge of the developmental patterns typical of young children in the preschool years, we have made **active learning** the cornerstone of our educational approach. By active learning, we mean learning that is initiated by the learner rather than "handed down" or "transmitted" by the teacher. For an activity to be judged active it must include the following five key ingredients:

☐ **Materials** — A variety of interesting materials are readily accessible to children.

☐ **Manipulation** — Children are free to handle, explore, and work with the materials.

☐ **Choice** — Children have opportunities to set their own goals and select materials and activities.

☐ **Language from the children** — Children talk about what they are doing and what they have done.

☐ **Support from adults** — Adults encourage the children's efforts and help them extend or build upon their work, by talking with them about what they are doing, by joining in their play, and by helping them solve problems that arise.

Why are opportunities to make choices emphasized so much in our approach to children's learning? In any early childhood program, children develop at different rates, and their interests and experiences vary widely. Yet teachers and caregivers often plan activities as if all their children were alike.

Consider, for example, the teacher who expects all 20 children in a group to sit down and color the letter *E* with a blue crayon. This teacher is assuming that all the children can color, that they all can recognize the color blue, and that they all are interested in this particular task. No wonder that during such activities far more child management statements are heard from adults than statements of pleasure or pride in children's work. However, when children are encouraged to make choices, they will initiate activities that grow from their personal interests and experiences. Such personally meaningful activities are usually a better starting point for learning than narrowly defined tasks imposed by an adult.

Room Arrangement

We feel strongly that children learn best in an environment that is stimulating but ordered — one in which they can make choices and act upon those choices. Thus the High/Scope Curriculum emphasizes careful attention to **arranging and equipping the classroom or center.** The environment is designed to encourage both social interaction and solitary play, and to provide comfortable spaces for both individual and group activities. To encourage children's self-reliance and purposeful play, the space is divided into **interest areas:** for example, house, art, block, and toy areas. Each area is stocked with a rich variety of materials, equipment, and tools; these materials are well organized, labelled, and accessible to children. Children know where materials are, and they can get them out and put them away without adult help.

Daily Routine

A predictable **daily routine** is another curriculum element that helps to provide an orderly framework for children's activities. The routine allows time for individual, small-group, and large-group activities and includes the following components:

Planning time. Adults meet with small groups of children to talk about what each child wants to do and how he or she may go about doing it. Children make decisions and adults encourage and support children as they clarify and develop their ideas.

Work time. This is the longest single time period in the daily routine. During this time, children carry out their original plans or choose new activities. They are free to work in all areas of the classroom, exploring materials, learning new skills, trying out their ideas, and putting together what they are learning in ways that make sense to them. Adults are equally active. They observe what interests the children and how children solve problems, and they seek ways to support children in developing their ideas. Adults help extend children's ideas in many ways: by working alongside them with similar materials, by joining in their role play, and by helping them solve problems that arise.

Recall time. Adults help children recall and talk about what they did during work time. Adults describe what they have seen children do and encourage them to attach language to their actions, making children more aware of their ideas and experiences and better able to draw upon them in the future.

Small-group time. In this teacher-initiated segment of the routine, adults plan activities and select materials based upon children's interests and developmental levels. Within the framework set by the adult, children are encouraged to initiate their own ideas. This is an important time for teachers to observe individual differences in the ways children respond to new materials or in the new ways they think about using familiar materials.

Circle time. This is the only segment of the routine in which all adults and children in the classroom are involved in the same activity at the same time. Typical circle time activities are songs, stories, movement activities, games, and so forth. Even though the activity is planned by the adults and children are expected to participate, there are still many opportunities for individual children to share their own ideas and for the whole group to make use of these ideas.

The High/Scope Key Experiences

As noted earlier, key experiences are another basic element of High/Scope's curriculum framework. *The key experiences are broadly defined activities and processes that use the important intellectual, social, and motor abilities emerging in the preschool years.* The key experiences serve as guideposts for teachers and caregivers in understanding child development, in planning activities for children, in observing how children interact with materials and with one another, and in discussing children's progress with parents. *It is important to note that the key experiences are interrelated: they are not meant to be applied piecemeal, and most effective learning activities contain more than one key experience.*

The key experiences are a valuable tool for preschool educators who want to help children master important concepts without directive teaching. The key experiences bring flexibility to High/Scope's curriculum framework: They help assure that a program is developmentally valid, but do not tie teachers and caregivers into a rigid sequence of preplanned lessons. Instead, they can be applied to a variety of activities that children and adults design on their own.

The key experiences are grouped in categories that indicate eight key areas of young children's learning: **active learning, language, representation, classification, seriation, number, spatial rela-**

tions, and **time.** Each of the following chapters highlights one of these groups of key experiences. *(For a complete listing of the key experiences, please turn the page.)*

How to Use This Book

Working and Planning as a Team

We recommend that adults in programs based on the High/Scope Curriculum use a **team approach** to teaching. For teams to be effective, *we recommend that all team members spend a portion of each day meeting together to review the previous day's activities and to plan for the next day.*

Why do we believe in the team approach? In any work situation you will find adults who differ in experiences, interests, and strengths. Our belief in the value of adults working as a team parallels our approach to supporting the development of young children. We believe that given the noncritical support of other members of the team, each adult's unique abilities and strengths will flourish.

But creating such a supportive team is not always easy. Many pressures in our schools and centers work against the effectiveness of teaching teams. For example, time to evaluate and plan together is often not set aside in the regular working day; adults teaching together in the same setting earn widely differing salaries; staff roles are often defined in a rigid or hierarchical way; individual work habits and personalities vary; and staff members have different philosophies about how children should be treated. While such problems might seem insurmountable, they are worth dealing with because the benefits to planning in a team far outweigh such problems.

What are these benefits? Some of them are listed below, along with "real-life" examples excerpted from a journal one teacher kept on her team-teaching experiences.

- ☐ ***Increased support and training for individual staff members.*** *"When six out of the nine children at Jackie's small group table wandered away five minutes into group time, we sat down to look at the reasons. After helping Jackie work through her feelings of disappointment in herself, we decided that in planning the activity, we had tried to introduce too many new materials at the same time. Next time we make fruit salad, we'll start by giving children bananas and raisins rather than four different types of fruit at once."*

- ☐ ***An opportunity for team members to learn from one another.*** *"Pat's picture-the-activity chart was a good idea. It was especially helpful to the children who were not yet familiar with the daily routine."*

- ☐ ***A forum for idea exchange and debate.*** *"We put a suggestion box up in the center. When we have questions we can't*

Key Experiences for Young Children

Key experiences in active learning

- ☐ Exploring actively with all the senses
- ☐ Discovering relationships through direct experience
- ☐ Manipulating, transforming, and combining materials
- ☐ Choosing materials, activities, and purposes
- ☐ Acquiring skills with tools and equipment
- ☐ Using the large muscles
- ☐ Taking care of one's own needs

Key experiences in using language

- ☐ Talking with others about personally meaningful experiences
- ☐ Describing objects, events, and relationships
- ☐ Expressing feelings in words
- ☐ Having one's own spoken language written down by an adult and read back
- ☐ Having fun with language: rhyming, making up stories, listening to poems and stories

Key experiences in representing experiences and ideas

- ☐ Recognizing objects by sound, touch, taste, and smell
- ☐ Imitating actions and sounds
- ☐ Relating pictures, photographs, and models to real places and things
- ☐ Role-playing, pretending
- ☐ Making models out of clay, blocks, etc.
- ☐ Drawing and painting
- ☐ Observing that spoken words can be written down and read back

Key experiences in developing logical reasoning

Classification

- ☐ Investigating and labeling the attributes of things
- ☐ Noticing and describing how things are the same and how they are different; sorting and matching
- ☐ Using and describing something in several different ways
- ☐ Distinguishing between "some" and "all"
- ☐ Holding more than one attribute in mind at a time
- ☐ Describing what characteristics something does *not* possess or what class it does *not* belong to

Seriation

☐ Comparing along a single dimension: bigger/smaller, heavier/lighter, rougher/smoother, louder/softer, harder/softer, longer/shorter, taller/shorter, wider/narrower, etc.
☐ Arranging several things in order along some dimension and describing the relationships (the longest one, the shortest one, etc.)
☐ Fitting one ordered set of objects to another through trial and error

Number

☐ Comparing number and amount: more/less, same amount
☐ Arranging two sets of objects in one-to-one correspondence
☐ Counting objects

Spatial Relations

☐ Fitting things together and taking them apart
☐ Rearranging and reshaping objects (folding, twisting, stretching, stacking, tying)
☐ Observing things and places from different spatial viewpoints
☐ Experiencing and describing relative positions, directions, and distances
☐ Experiencing and representing one's own body
☐ Learning to locate things in the classroom, school, and neighborhood
☐ Interpreting representations of spatial relations in drawings and pictures
☐ Distinguishing and describing shapes

Time

Understanding Time Units or Intervals

☐ Stopping and starting an action on signal
☐ Experiencing and describing different rates of speed
☐ Experiencing and comparing time intervals
☐ Observing seasonal changes
☐ Observing that clocks and calendars are used to mark the passage of time

Sequencing Events in Time

☐ Anticipating future events verbally and making appropriate preparations
☐ Planning and completing what one has planned
☐ Describing and representing past events
☐ Using conventional time units in talking about past and future events
☐ Noticing, describing, and representing the order of events

Key experiences in understanding time and space

answer, we write them down and drop them in the box. Then we meet as a group and analyze them together."

☐ ***A cooperative approach to problem-solving.*** *"There is a problem with the room arrangement that has been bothering Jackie and me. We seem to need more room in the housekeeping area — so we decided that tomorrow, when the kids are off, we'll make the quiet area smaller and enlarge the housekeeping area."*

Making Your Daily Plan

This book can help you in the daily process of team planning. (Though we strongly recommend planning *daily,* some teams are unable to do this. In this case, we recommend group planning *one or more times a week.* If you are not teaching in a team, this book can still provide helpful suggestions for planning.)

We suggest that team members pick one of the groups of key experiences to focus on for the entire day or week. You might also choose a content theme (for example, special celebrations, springtime, families). As you discuss plans for carrying out the key experiences and themes selected, we suggest jotting down ideas for each of the major parts of the daily routine: planning, work time, recall, small-group, and circle time. You can consult this book and other High/Scope curriculum materials for ideas as you plan. In using the strategies in this book, note that many of the suggestions given for one part of the routine may be easily adapted for another. For example, most of the ideas for planning time can also be used at recall time.

Next, try out your plan. Remember that plans should be flexible. Don't be afraid to modify or abandon a planned activity. When in doubt, follow the children's lead, keeping your focus for the day in mind, but moving in a completely new direction if warranted. For example, during the first new snow of the season, you may find children staring out the window instead of participating in your small-group activity. In this case you may decide to change your plan and use the snow as a learning experience.

We suggest that the team review the day's experiences when planning for the next day. Discuss your observations about individual children, jotting down notes about their accomplishments. You may also note which teaching strategies worked and which didn't, and how you would modify a strategy the next time you use it. (You might even note such modifications in the margins of this book.) Then develop a plan for the next day that follows up on the day's observations while introducing new themes, concepts, or materials. Going through this planning process for each day's program may seem like a tall order for busy teachers and caregivers, but many teachers we've trained say that once they get in the habit of planning, it makes their work with children easier.

In Appendix A we give a sample plan developed by one teaching team using the process we've described here and many of the teaching strategies recommended in this book. The key experience focus this team chose was spatial relations; they also decided to highlight the ad-

ditional theme of springtime. Since one can't always predict how plans
will work out, the sample plan also includes the observations the teaching team made when they discussed how the plan worked out at their
next planning session.

High/Scope Observation and Assessment Tools

In addition to this book, another High/Scope resource that is useful in
the planning process is our Child Assessment Record (CAR). The CAR
is an observation record that teachers fill out on each child, making
brief, specific notations on a child's accomplishments in the major key
experience areas. Typically, each teaching team member makes several
such notations each day on a few children's CARs. (It would be far too
time-consuming to record something every day on every child.) Peri-
odically, notations on the CAR are used as the basis for filling out the
Child Observation Record (COR), a detailed assessment instrument
that is compiled once or twice a year. A sample of a filled-out CAR is
provided in Appendix B. For more information on using these observation and assessment tools, we recommend attending a High/Scope
workshop on assessment.

   Additional resources that may be useful when planning are the
books listed in Appendix C. Most of the songs and fingerplays men-
tioned in the text are given in these books; also included are many
more songs, chants, and fingerplays that can be used with or adapted
to the strategies suggested in each chapter.

*   *   *   *   *

   Now that we have introduced the basics of our curriculum
approach and explained our team planning process, we move to the
practical teaching strategies that we promised earlier. Each of the
following chapters focuses on a group of key experiences, presenting
specific strategies for applying these key experiences in your daily work
with children. Please use these ideas in the spirit in which we present
them — as suggestions to spark your own thinking about how to make
your classroom, home, or center a place where children's ideas and
language can flourish.

ACTIVE LEARNING

Active learning is the process by which young children explore the world: observing; listening; searching; moving their bodies; touching, smelling, handling, and making things happen with the objects around them. Children who are actively learning pursue goals that are important to them and organize their discoveries in unique ways. As they explore, they construct unique conceptions of the world, conceptions that may not correspond to the adult view of reality.

Active learning is a natural process. Teaching adults and caregivers can't force it to happen, but they can create the conditions that make it possible. You can test whether a learning experience is truly active by noting whether it contains the five **ingredients of active learning** described in the introductory chapter: materials, manipulation, choice, language from the children, and support from adults. The following **key experiences in active learning** can serve as a guide for all your planning and teaching:

- ☐ Exploring actively with all the senses
- ☐ Discovering relationships through direct experience
- ☐ Manipulating, transforming, and combining materials
- ☐ Choosing materials, activities, and purposes
- ☐ Acquiring skills with tools and equipment
- ☐ Using the large muscles
- ☐ Taking care of one's own needs

A child who is encouraged to use tools and equipment to take care of his own needs is developing a lifelong capacity for self-reliance.

Note that while most of the other key experiences focus on specific concepts, the active learning key experiences are broader, describing processes that should be present in *all* classroom activities. Even so, it is helpful from time to time to focus specifically on these key experiences. Following are suggestions for supporting active learning at specific times in your daily routine.

Planning Time

1. Ask one or two children to bring an object they will work with to the planning table while the others close their eyes. Give children chances to explore the object with their senses — to touch it, smell it, and listen to the sounds it makes — and to guess what the object might be.

2. Encourage children to share their ideas on different ways they can use their bodies to get to the areas they have selected to work in: for example, hopping, crawling, jumping, taking giant steps. Then have them move to their chosen area in one of these ways.

3. Help children develop their plans beyond just naming the areas they will work in. Encourage them to think about which materials and equipment they will use and the ways they will manipulate, transform, and combine them: "How will you use the play dough? [Pause for response.] What will you do with your fingers? [Pause.] How might you use the cookie cutters with the play dough?"

4. Choose one or two children to bring the materials they have selected for work time to the planning table and ask them to demonstrate how they will use them: "Nancy, your plan is to make a picture with glue. Could you show the other children how your fingers will squeeze the glue bottle?"

5. Help children think about ways they can combine materials to accomplish their plans. For example, if a child's plan is to "make a house in the block area," you might ask, "Will there be enough room in your house for the babies from the house area to sleep there?"

Acquiring skills with tools and equipment gives children the feeling that they are in charge.

1. Stock your areas with *real* items, for example: full-size plastic plates, silverware, telephones, toasters, and plastic pitchers.

2. Have living things (small animals, fish, house plants, sprouted seeds) in your classroom, home, or center, and have children take turns being responsible for their care.

3. Sit beside a child and play with materials yourself as you watch the child play. For example, if you see a child using inch-cube blocks in the toy area, you could sit next to him with your own set of blocks and begin building. Talk about what *you* are doing. You may also model new ways of manipulating, transforming, and combining materials, without pressuring the child to imitate you or to change his or her own ideas.

4. Encourage children to follow through on their ideas and take care of their own needs as independently as possible. For example, if a child's plan is to work with the clothing in the house area, encourage her to button, snap, lace, and zip the clothing herself. If you notice that she's about to abandon her plan because she can't get a button buttoned, try talking her through the process instead of doing it for her: "Push the button through the hole and then pull it out on the other side." Allow children to replenish supplies as they run out: "The tape dispenser is empty. Here is a box with a new roll of tape that you can use to fill it again."

5. Encourage children to use their large muscles within the context of their chosen activities: "I see you are all dressed up to go to the party. Will you have dancing at your party?"

6. Plan for large-motor activities as you set up the interest areas. For example, make the block area large enough for children to move around in and crawl through spaces; if possible, make the music area spacious enough for children to move to music or to set up a stage for singing in it.

7. Continually evaluate the tools and equipment in your areas in terms of children's abilities to use them with success. Materials should be in good repair and appropriate for the age group you serve. For example, ask yourself, "Are these scissors safe and will they enhance children's cutting skills?" "Can the children operate the school record player without damaging its parts? Would a tape recorder be more durable?"

8. Add the flannel-board story pieces introduced during circle time to classroom interest areas. Encourage children to explore and manipulate the pieces and to create their own stories.

Simple equipment offers challenging opportunities to use the large muscles.

9. When children are working at classroom computers, avoid the temptation to step in and "do it for them" when a problem arises. Instead, use language that encourages children to take care of their own needs: "Why don't you see what happens when you press this key?" "I see your picture tore when you tried to tear the computer paper along the line. I noticed that when Bonnie had that problem she used scissors to get her picture out of the printer."

10. Select computer programs that support active learning by encouraging the child's experimentation, choice, and creative input. For example, the drawing and coloring program *Color Me* from Mindscape, Inc., allows children to draw whatever they want on the computer screen with a "mouse," to choose colors, and to add letters or words to their pictures.

ACTIVE LEARNING
Recall Time

1. Collect toys that you have observed children using during work time. Bring them to the recall table and allow children to explore them in different ways. Encourage them to talk about the different ways they used the materials: "Troy used these Legos to build a tall tower. What other things could you do with them? [Pause for response.] What kind of sound will they make if you hit them together?"

2. Question children about additional materials they might use to expand upon their work-time activities: "If you plan to work on your rocket ship tomorrow, what materials would you need to finish it?"

3. Encourage children to use their large muscles by mimicking, with exaggerated motion, the work-time activities of other children: "Vanessa said she painted at the easel. Let's all pretend that we're painting at the easel and that it is very, very big. How would our arms move if we wanted to cover the whole picture?"

ACTIVE LEARNING
Small-Group Time

1. In the early part of the year, plan small-group times to introduce the materials in each of the classroom areas. For example, plan sessions on Bristle Blocks, different kinds of paints and paper, and sand area materials. This will help children be aware of the choices available to them at work time and will introduce them to the skills needed to use tools, equipment, and materials effectively.

These children are discovering relationships through direct experience.

2. Turn a long mirror on its side at the table. Give each child a toothbrush, toothpaste, and a paper cup half full of water. Let them watch themselves brushing their teeth. Make comments like "Look at how the water changed colors when you put your toothbrush in." Ask questions like "How does your mouth taste now that you've brushed your teeth?"

3. Collect enough net-type potato or onion bags so that each child has one. Add yarn pieces and encourage children to explore and combine the materials (for example, by sewing in and out of the holes in the netting with yarn).

4. Making a fruit salad is a simple activity that allows children to gain skill with safe cutting tools (use blunt table knives) as well as to explore and combine interesting materials. Start with soft fruits like bananas and peaches that children can easily cut themselves. Progress to firmer fruits like oranges and apples.

Making scrambled eggs is an opportunity to manipulate, transform, and combine materials.

5. Give each child a large plastic bag filled with partially crushed ice. Let them use blocks, hammers, or rubber mallets to crush the ice further. Then have them pour the crushed ice into a cup, and encourage them to pour fruit juice over it for a refreshing warm-weather snack.

6. Spread a large piece of paper on the floor. Give each child paint and a piece of string and let them string paint using large arm movements: "Karl, can you stretch your painting string over to the other side to where Carlos is sitting?"

7. Take the children outside to rake fall leaves, giving each child his or her own rake. Ask questions and make comments that encourage children to discover relationships as they explore with all their senses: "How do your arms feel now that you've raked the leaves into a big pile?" "Listen to the sound the leaves make when you walk on top of them." "I wonder if the brown leaves smell the same as the orange ones." "Some of the leaves are wet and some are dry. Which are easier for you to rake?"

ACTIVE LEARNING

Circle Time

1. Vary traditional songs by allowing children to choose ways to change the lyrics. For example, for "There were ten in the bed and the little one said 'Roll over,' " ask: "What else could the little one do, besides roll over? [Pause for response.] That's a good idea. The little one could *jump over* [hop over, skip over]. Let's sing it that way."

2. Have a weekly exercise circle or plan on spending some time during each circle time in gross-motor activities.

3. Tell flannel-board stories in which children can be involved in placing the pieces as they appear in the story.

4. Sing "This-A-Way, That-A-Way, Any Old Way" with the children. Have children choose what motions to do.

LANGUAGE

When books are made available in a quiet part of the classroom, children can escape into the world of stories.

Children's language abilities will develop naturally in a classroom environment rich in opportunities for both **oral and written communication.** To create such a setting, encourage children to talk about what they plan to do, what they are doing, and what they did, both to adults and other children. As children talk about their experiences, help them develop the complexity of their language by repeating, interpreting, and building upon their statements. Listening attentively is another important language skill, one that you can encourage in children by modeling it yourself. Encouraging children to have fun with language through puns, jokes, rhyming games, play with nonsense words, and made-up songs and stories is another way to build language skills and make children aware of the pleasures of using words.

Experiences with written language should not be separate from other classroom activities but should grow naturally from the rich flow of communication in the classroom. You can help children become aware of the value of writing and reading by including written language in the environment: by making books and writing materials freely available, and by including words, along with pictures, symbols, or outlines, in some of your labels for toys and equipment. It is also important to read frequently to children, and to take dictation throughout the daily routine. You should also encourage children to make written language a part of their pretend play; for example, suggest that they "write" grocery lists, traffic tickets, letters, recipes, or signs, and then use such common forms of writing yourself when you join in their role play.

When children are interested and ready, you can help them write a few letters and words by giving them models to trace or copy. Provide personal word boxes in which children can store favorite words that they can recognize by sight. If children are interested, you may point out phonics or spelling facts as you read back their dictations, but avoid pushing academic learning prematurely with language worksheets, letter or phonics drills, or writing exercises. Letter recognition and phonics skills may be conveyed within the context of ongoing activities, but only if children are ready.

By stressing the **meaning,** rather than the **mechanics,** of written language, you will provide a strong base for the development of later

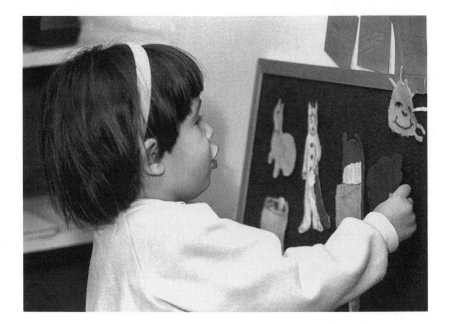

After introducing a flannel-board story at circle time, make it available in the toy area so children can retell the story as they play with the pieces.

academic skills. Use the following **key experiences in language** as the basis for classroom activities that encourage children to communicate verbally:

☐ Talking with others about personally meaningful experiences
☐ Describing objects, events, and relationships
☐ Expressing feelings in words
☐ Having one's own spoken language written down by an adult and read back
☐ Having fun with language: rhyming, making up stories, listening to poems and stories

LANGUAGE

Planning Time

1. Start planning time by asking one or two children to describe their work from the day before. It will be easier for the other children if you choose someone who has made something that can also be shared visually, such as a painting or Lego structure. Ask the others if they would like to make a plan to play with the same materials.

2. Tell a story with Teddy Bear Counters and inch-cube blocks about a school called [insert the name of your center or school] where the children make plans. Give each child a bear and ask him or her to describe what she or he would like to do that day.

3. Use nonsense rhymes with the children: "Oh, you're going to play with the *Teddy Bear Counters.* That rhymes with *Weddy Wear Wounters.*" Older children may enjoy giving others a rhyming clue and then asking them to guess their plan: "Today I want to play in the *mouse area*" [for house area].

4. When appropriate, take dictation from children about their plans. These plans may range from one word to several sentences.

5. Encourage children who plan to work in the same area together to talk through those plans with each other before they begin work: "Lauretta, your plan is to cook in the house area, and so is Samuel's. What can you tell each other about what you are planning to cook?"

6. Use props like tape recorders, puppets, telephones, walkie-talkies, and microphones to encourage children to describe their plans as fully as they are able.

Taking dictation from children and reading it back helps them recognize the connection between written and spoken language.

1. Encourage children to talk with other children whenever possible during work time: "Jessica, I'm talking to Andrea at the easel right now. Could you please tell Jason how to make the stapler work?"

2. When conflicts occur, encourage children to notice and describe each other's reactions: "Benjamin, look at Alicia's face. What does it look like?"

LANGUAGE

Work Time

3. Encourage children to describe their own feelings. "You said you couldn't hang up your own picture to dry, but I see that you really did. How does that make you feel?"

4. Listen carefully to children when they talk to you. Get down at their level, make eye contact, and look at the objects they are showing you. If you are distracted, explain to them that you're sorry and can't listen because another child needs your help.

5. Asking children to give you directions is one way to encourage them to describe what they have done: "That's a tall building. Tell me how you made it so I can make one, too."

6. Have a variety of reading materials available for children to look at and listen to. Put books, flannel-board stories, newspapers, photographs, and magazines in the book area.

7. Take dictation on children's work: "What part of the house did you say this was? The roof — I'll write that word down . . . Is there anything else you want me to write down about your house?"

8. Add a tape recorder to the book area. Have blank tapes available for children to use to record and listen to their own voices. Record your own voice reading some of the familiar stories you have in the classroom and have these tapes available for children to listen to and enjoy.

9. Create a writing center. Stock it with wooden, plastic, and sand-paper letters for children to explore and trace. Add different writing implements and paper. If possible, bring in a working typewriter or a computer.

10. Select computer programs that foster children's interest in letters by allowing them to explore letter shapes, for example, *Kid's Stuff* from Stone & Associates.

11. Encourage older children who are interested in and ready for writing to use the computer to write and to listen to their own words as spoken by the computer. Several programs turn the computer into a talking word processor that reads aloud what the child types, for example, *Dr. Peet's Talk Writer* from Hartley Courseware, Inc., and *Talking Text Writer* from Scholastic, Inc. Such programs provide large letters that are easy for preschoolers to recognize on the screen.

12. When children are working at a computer, use language to label what they are doing: "I see. You're pressing the spacebar to move the cursor."

13. When a child working at a computer asks an adult for help, encourage him or her to use language to find out how another child solved the same problem: "Josh, can you ask Erin how she got her picture out of the printer?"

LANGUAGE

Recall Time

1. Use a puppet as you describe what you saw the children doing: "I was watching Louie build a tall tower in the block area today. He cried when it got knocked over." Give each child a puppet to continue the conversation with your puppet.

2. Play back a tape recording of children's work time plans (made during planning time). Encourage the children to talk about their plans: "On the tape you said you were going to paint a picture. Did you do that? [Pause for response.] Will you bring it to the table and tell the other children about it?"

3. Give children crayons and paper to draw a picture of something they did at work time or to trace around an object they used. Take dictation about what they did (writing directly on their pictures), put the children's pictures in a book, and put the book in the book area.

LANGUAGE

Small-Group Time

1. Provide a variety of materials for making puppets. If this is the first time you've introduced puppet-making, start simply, with small lunch sacks and crayons, for example. Later in the year, or for older children, you can conduct the activity with additional materials: items for pasting, newspapers for stuffing, toilet paper rolls of different sizes, old socks. As the children choose materials and assemble them, listen to them and converse with them. When the puppets are finished, encourage children to make them "talk."

2. Bring a variety of materials children can choose from to make special occasion cards. Encourage children to leave space on their cards to write their own messages or for you to write down their dictated messages.

3. After returning from field trips, encourage children to draw what they remember about the trip. Ask them what they would like to say to the people they visited, write down their statements, and assemble the pictures and statements on a giant thank-you card. Use the same process to make giant cards for children who are sick and absent from school, or for friends and family members on birthdays and other special occasions.

4. Have each child choose a large handful of Teddy Bear Counters and several large wooden or plastic letters. As children experiment with how the bears fit in and around the letters, listen to what they have to say and converse with them about what they are doing: "You fit the bears into a circle all around the letter O." "Look what happens when you turn the *T* upside down. You can only fit one bear at the top."

These children are experimenting with Teddy Bear Counters and large wooden letters as in suggestion 4.

5. Take the children to one of the interest areas. Let them explore the materials in that area. As they work, be available to listen to the ways they describe materials and to converse with them about what you see them doing.

6. Have the group make up a story together while transcribing it for them on the computer. Start by introducing a theme, such as "What We Saw and Did at the Park," and ask each child to make up a part of the story, taking down each child's dictation on the computer and including each child's name on his or her part of the story. To avoid long waits as you are taking dictation, give children crayons and paper to illustrate their ideas. When the story is done, print it out and read it back to the children, asking for their help as you read. Make copies to send home with children, attaching children's illustrations, so that parents can read the story with their children at home.

1. Make up songs with children in which you and they describe different actions for everyone to imitate: "What can you do to get your sillies out, Joshua? [Joshua stamps his feet.] What's that called?" [Pause for response.] "Stomping," says another child. "Oh, *stomping*. Okay, let's sing. Stomp, stomp, stomp your sillies out; Stomp, stomp, stomp your sillies out; Stomp, stomp, stomp your sillies out; Wiggle your waggles away."

2. Ask children for ways to adapt the song, "If You're Happy and You Know It," to include other feelings and actions: "If you're angry and you know it, shake your head."

3. Sing the song, "Willouby, Wallouby, Woo, An Elephant Sat on You," adding rhymes using the children's names. Keeping the initial consonant sound the same will make this easier for the children: "Willouby, Wallouby, *Wancy,* An elephant sat on *Nancy.*" "Willouby, Willouby *Wuth,* An elephant sat on *Ruth.*" As the children learn the song, ask them for their own ideas for other rhymes.

4. Play the "Let's Be" game. Have the children take turns describing someone or something for everyone else to pretend to be: "Let's pretend we're painting a giant building." "Let's pretend we're a puppy dog excited to see our owner."

5. Read aloud the dictated stories the children created when they were recalling field trip experiences.

6. Read stories to the children. To keep things interesting, vary the approach by using picture books or flannel-board stories, and by planning ways for children to talk about or act out parts of the story: "Can you shake both hands like the monkeys did?"

REPRESENTATION

The ability to **represent the world** in a variety of ways — through drawing, model-making, block building, pretending, song, dance, and language, for example — is one of the most important areas of learning in the preschool years. As young children depict their experiences in these tangible ways, they are also developing the capacity to mentally represent their experiences. In Piaget's theory, this capacity to form mental images eventually becomes integrated with other reasoning processes to produce adult capacities for symbolic and creative thinking.

The first stage in the development of preschoolers' abilities to **interpret representations** involves learning to recognize "sensory cues," the sounds, smells, tastes, or textures that "stand for" an object when it is not present or visible (examples: a bootprint in the snow, an ambulance siren, the click of a key in the front-door lock). Children take another step forward in the development of their representational abilities when they become aware that books and drawings are symbolic of "real" things in the world. Though even very young children enjoy stories, they often don't realize that the pictures in the books are not real objects. A third, more complex, stage in the development of children's abilities to interpret representations is learning to decode such formal symbols as numerals, letters, and words.

Children's ability to **produce representations** also develops gradually, starting with simple imitation and slowly moving to more elaborate pretending and the production of simple drawings, paintings, and models. As preschoolers' ability to represent develops, they may be able to produce their own simple writing.

When planning for representational activities, remember that preschoolers' abilities to interpret representations and to produce representations develop gradually. Start by having them work with concrete representations of ongoing activities or very recent experiences. Then move gradually to more abstract, symbolic representations of past or future experiences. Encourage children to represent during planning or recall time, and offer a wide variety of materials and media that can be used for representation throughout the day. Encourage children to increase the complexity of their representations by participating in their role play; by working alongside them as they draw, paint, and build;

By acting out their experiences in dramatic play, children develop the capacity for symbolic and creative thought.

and by questioning them about their representations. Use the following **key experiences in representing experiences and ideas** as your guide in working with children:

- ☐ Recognizing objects by sound, touch, taste, and smell
- ☐ Imitating actions and sounds
- ☐ Relating pictures, photographs, and models to real places and things
- ☐ Role-playing, pretending
- ☐ Making models out of clay, blocks, etc.
- ☐ Drawing and painting
- ☐ Observing that spoken words can be written down and read back

REPRESENTATION

Planning Time

1. To incorporate role play into planning time, make several walkie-talkies or telephones using classroom materials, such as Legos or wooden blocks. Call children, one at a time, and ask them to tell you their plans over their walkie-talkie or telephone: "Calling firefighter Bill, calling firefighter Bill. Can you pick up your walkie-talkie and tell me your plan?"

2. To help children make the connection between pictures and real things, give each child a large piece of blank paper. Ask each child to bring one object they will use at work time to the table to trace around. Converse with children about their objects and plans as they trace, and take dictation if appropriate.

3. Cut pictures out of catalogs or magazines of materials available in your classroom, or take photographs of them. As children talk about their plans, have them choose a picture of one thing they will work with. This is another way of giving children the opportunity to relate pictures to real things.

4. Make area symbol cards that represent the work or interest areas of the classroom. Have children pick the card for the area they want to work in. *(See photo.)*

5. Using pictures of materials in your classroom (suggestion 3) and the area symbols (suggestion 4), make a central planning board on which children can record their plans by using their own symbols, the area symbols, and the pictures of materials. Strips of Velcro on the backs of the pictures can be used to fasten them to the board. *(See drawing.)*

Make area symbol cards to represent the interest areas of your classroom. Let children select them at planning time to show in which area they plan to work.

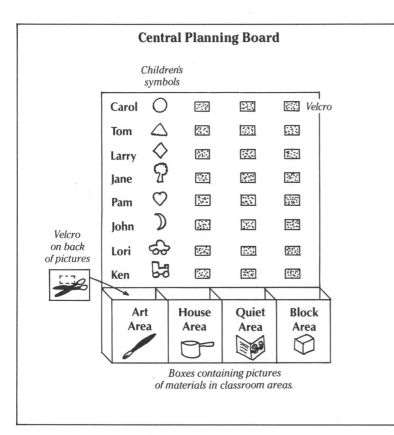

Central Planning Board

Children's symbols

Carol	◯	▨	▨	▨ *Velcro*
Tom	△	▨	▨	▨
Larry	◇	▨	▨	▨
Jane	♣	▨	▨	▨
Pam	♡	▨	▨	▨
John	☾	▨	▨	▨
Lori	⚙	▨	▨	▨
Ken	⚙	▨	▨	▨

Velcro on back of pictures

Art Area	House Area	Quiet Area	Block Area

Boxes containing pictures of materials in classroom areas.

Children can use a central planning board to represent their plans.

6. Make planning forms with line drawings representing the interest areas. Have children fill in or color the area they will work in.

7. On blank planning forms, ask children to draw pictures of what they will do or of the materials they will use. *(See photo.)*

Encourage children to represent their plans on blank planning forms. This child's planning form shows a picture of a computer with the words *computer area.*

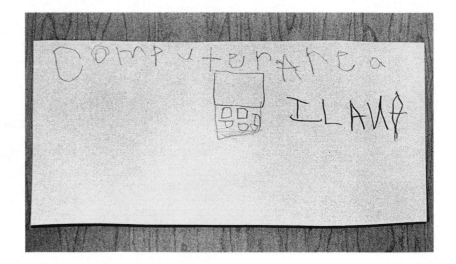

REPRESENTATION

Work Time

1. To encourage role play, add prop boxes to the house area. Include props and clothing on a particular theme inside the box; label the outside with pictures and words. For example, a grocery store box could be labelled with pictures or photos of a check-out clerk, bag stuffer, meat cutter, and customers. Inside, it might contain a toy cash register, empty food containers, play money, paper bags, and a long, white butcher's apron.

2. Put toy cameras or nonworking real cameras in the house area. Encourage children to "develop" their pictures by drawing what they see through the lens.

3. To encourage children to draw and dictate, add a book-making area to the classroom. Include hole punches, staplers, yarn, cardboard, glue, markers, magazines, and paper. (See also work-time suggestion 9, *Language.*)

4. Join in children's role play and help them extend their representational activities. For example, if a child is pretending to fish, you might suggest building a fire to cook the fish. This encourages children to find something to represent (stand for) the fuel and the flames.

5. Help children link their role play activities with those of others: "Angelina, I see you're all dressed up to go shopping. I wonder if the bus Kerry built in the block area is going in your direction?"

6. Take "instant" photographs of children at their work-time activities. Use them to discuss with children the real things they stand for.

7. To help children see the connection between real babies and baby dolls, invite parents to bring their babies to school. Have children participate, as much as possible, in bathing, diapering, or feeding the baby. Stock your house area with baby dolls and watch to see how children reenact their experiences with the real babies.

8. Enter into children's role play situations by assuming a role that is relevant to what is happening — patient, next-door neighbor, bus driver, and so forth. For example, if you want to join children who are playing doctor and nurse, enter quietly, and explain that you woke up with a stomachache and were hoping to see the doctor.

9. To support and encourage role play, take local field trips (grocery store, fire station, pizza parlor, park, farm, staff member's home). Bring back items to add to the interest areas (fireman's hat, pizza pan, order forms) that will help children add realistic details to their play.

After a trip to the fire station, children reenact their experience in play.

10. Encourage children to draw pictures of their activities. For example, if a child is building a block tower, you might suggest that she draw a picture of a tower. Or you might pretend to take a picture of the tower, then make a sketch of it and present it to the child.

11. To prepare for a recall time that gives children the opportunity to recognize people and objects by the sounds they make, tape record what children are saying and the noises they make as they play in the interest areas.

12. Stock your art area with a variety of paper and paints so children can experiment with the process of painting. Think beyond paintbrushes to painting with corks, pine branches, Q-tips, sponges, and so forth.

13. To give children experience with model-making, make available supplies that can be used for three-dimensional representations. For example, children enjoy using play dough, boxes, bottlecaps, pipecleaners, blocks, and popsicle sticks to make pretend pizzas, houses, airplanes, and other representations of real objects.

14. Make available the computer program *Mask Parade* from Springboard. This program allows children to make masks, hats, and jewelry on the computer screen and then to print them out in life size. Children can then take these printouts to the art area, decorate them, cut them out, and attach them to headbands, strings, or tape so that they can wear them. These costume materials can then be used for dress up or role play.

REPRESENTATION
Recall Time

1. Play back tape recordings made at work time. Have children listen to the sounds and voices and guess which children were playing and what materials they were using.

2. Collect objects children used at work time and put them under a blanket or in a large bag or container. Encourage them to identify the objects by touching and feeling them.

3. Encourage children to make models of what they did at work time using play dough, toothpicks and clay, or other materials. Talk with children about how they used the objects they are representing.

4. Bring paintings and models children have made during work time and encourage them to demonstrate and describe how they made their creations.

5. Ask children to show others what they did at work time without using words. For example, they may pantomime an activity or point to the materials they used. Encourage the other children to imitate the pantomimer's actions and to guess the activity it represents.

6. Bring a large sheet of paper to the recall table. Start by saying, "Today I saw someone playing with something that looks like this." (Sketch the easel, a tinkertoy, or other materials you saw a child use.) Ask children to guess what your picture is and then ask the child who played with that material to talk about what she or he did with it at work time.

7. Encourage children to use classroom computers to represent what they did at work time. Drawing programs such as *Color Me* from Mindscape, Inc., enable children to draw a picture related to something they made or a material they used. If children are interested and ready, they can also use such a program to add labels and descriptions to their pictures, or the teacher can add words dictated by the child.

1. Plan a series of small-group times in which children can make models with scrap wood. In the first small-group time, provide the wood scraps and encourage children to explore, experiment, or build with them. For the next small-group time, add one or two kinds of fasteners (glue, yarn, hammer and nails, tape) that children can use to fasten their wood pieces together. In the third small-group time, provide chalk, crayons, markers, or paints and encourage children to decorate their wood-scrap structures or models.

2. Give each child a bag filled with inch-cube blocks and Teddy Bear Counters to play with. Watch to see which children explore and build with the materials and which children pretend with them. After they've done this small-group time one or two times, you may vary it by beginning with a story about a school named [insert the name of your center or school] with lots of children and toys to play with. Use the blocks and bears to role play as you tell the story. Observe whether or not your story encourages the children who have been exploring with the materials to try out some role play ideas with the blocks and bears.

3. Provide children with play dough and a variety of cookie cutters. As children cut shapes out of the play dough, talk with them about the pictures the cookie cutters make.

4. Encourage children to represent objects by putting them under paper and doing crayon rubbings. When everyone has finished, put all the objects in the middle of the table and encourage children to match the objects with the rubbings made from them.

REPRESENTATION

Small-Group Time

5. Do foot and hand painting. For example, encourage children and adults to dip their hands or feet in paint and print on or walk across a large piece of paper. Compare sizes of handprints and footprints, ask children to guess whose hand or foot made each print, and encourage them to match their hands or feet to their own prints. This helps children make the connection between their hands and the representations of their hands.

6. Give children opportunities to draw on surfaces other than paper (for example, by using chalk on large, unrestricted outdoor surfaces such as wood, concrete, bricks, asphalt, or stones).

7. During or after a snowfall or on a rainy day, give children Q-tips, white paint, and dark paper. Observe to see if children use the materials to represent the snow or rain.

8. To give children the opportunity to interpret representations, give each child an old toy catalog or the advertising sections of local newspapers. Converse with them about the pictures that are particularly interesting to them. If a child is very quiet, try initiating a conversation: "I really like the grapes on this page the best. What picture do you like?"

REPRESENTATION

Circle Time

1. Sit on the floor with children and pat your head (or any other part of your body). Encourage children to imitate you. When all the children are patting their heads, start to pat a different part of the body, for example, your knees. Again, encourage the children to imitate you. After a few rounds, encourage children to take turns being the leader. You can do this activity either with or without music.

2. Sing the song "Everybody Do This," and encourage each child to take a turn choosing an action for everyone else to imitate.

3. Read aloud books and stories children have dictated, and have children choose parts and act them out.

Imitating the actions of others is a representational activity that children enjoy at circle time.

CLASSIFICATION

Classification, the ability to sort or classify objects according to their attributes, is a basic logical skill that is developing during the preschool years. A child is classifying when he puts all the toy trucks together in the same box, when he sorts buttons into categories, or when he points out that he is no longer one of the three-year-olds.

A developmental milestone that occurs before classification is the child's making what Piaget called **graphic collections.** These are carefully arranged sets of objects that do not appear to have been selected according to their similarities or differences, or by any other rationale that makes sense to adults. As children grow older, however, they begin to notice and describe the **attributes** of objects: their shape, color, texture, size, weight, and so forth. They also begin to notice and compare **similarities** and **differences** among objects and to **sort** and **match** objects by consistent criteria; for example, a child might put all the blue blocks together, or all the broken crayons in one pile.

While most preschoolers quickly become adept at sorting and classifying objects according to one attribute (all objects that are brown, for example), considering two attributes at the same time (all objects that are brown and fuzzy) is much more difficult for them. While children may have no difficulty repeating two or three adjectives that describe an object, they may not be able to carry out an activity that requires them to think about all these characteristics at once. For example, after hearing a story about a brown and furry bear, a preschooler may be able to repeat that the bear was brown and furry. However, she may have great difficulty finding anything else in the room that is both brown and furry. Children can't be drilled or taught to think about two things simultaneously, but they can profit from hearing adults describe objects, situations, and events that are both one thing and another.

Children have a natural interest in classifying. You can help them develop this important thinking skill by planning activities with the following **key experiences in classification** in mind:

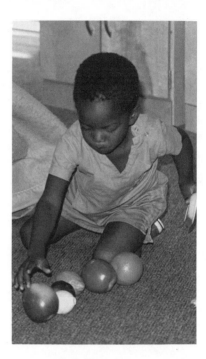

Classification skills develop as children begin to group objects according to their similarities and differences.

- ☐ Investigating and labeling the attributes of things
- ☐ Noticing and describing how things are the same and how they are different; sorting and matching
- ☐ Using and describing something in several different ways
- ☐ Distinguishing between "some" and "all"
- ☐ Holding more than one attribute in mind at a time
- ☐ Describing what characteristics something does *not* possess or what class it does *not* belong to

CLASSIFICATION

Planning Time

1. For each child in your planning group, find a pair of identical objects — for example, two purple crayons, two paper triangles, two unit blocks, and so forth. Collect one object from each pair and arrange them around the planning table, one for each child's space. Before the children come to the table, give each child one of the remaining objects that matches one that is already at the table. Start planning when everyone has found the match for his or her object. Some children may include their objects in their plans.

2. Place some objects that children often use at work time on the table. Ask each child if they can find something on the table that is *the same* as something they plan to use during work time.

3. Play a guessing game with the children. Ask them to get one thing they plan to use at work time, put it into a grocery bag, and bring it back to the table. Take turns having each child describe his or her object. (The child can look into his or her bag at the object, but the other children cannot). The child who is describing removes the object from his or her bag when another child guesses what it is.

4. When children verbally state their plans, ask them if they think it will take them *all* of work time or just *part* of work time to finish.

5. Pass out to older children a sheet with the symbols for the interest areas on it. (They should already be familiar with these symbols because you have referred to them repeatedly at planning and work times.) Ask children to cross out the areas they will *not* work in.

6. Ask two or three children to stand up. Say something like "The first person today to tell us their plan will be the person with green pants [or whatever attribute is unique to one of the three standing children]." As these children begin their activity, repeat the strategy with two or three others.

7. Ask children to go to the areas they will work in and bring back one thing they will work with that is light and one that is *heavy (smooth/ rough, round/not round, flat/bumpy).*

CLASSIFICATION

Work Time

1. Describe for children the attributes of objects they have selected to work with: "I see you're working with the wooden letters. Some of them have straight edges and some of them have rounded edges."

2. Model alternative ways to use materials and comment when you see children using materials in several different ways: "Marilyn, you're rolling your play dough between your hands. Jackie's squeezing his play dough through his fingers. I'm going to put mine on the table and press down on it."

Questions like "What can you tell me about that part" encourage children to notice and describe the attributes of objects.

By actively using and describing the same object in several different ways, these children are developing a basic logical reasoning skill.

3. Encourage children to sort: "Well, this soup smells good, but I really only like the bottlecaps and not the corks. Could you fix my bowl with just the things I like, while I set the table?"

4. Encourage children to match: "I'm going to string all yellow beads on my necklace. How are you going to make yours?"

5. Observe to see which children can hold more than one attribute in mind at a time. "Japera, could you please pass me that long, skinny piece of paper for my picture? I can't quite reach it."

6. Put unusual materials in your areas that invite children to notice and comment on their attributes. For example, add gourds to the house area in the fall. Listen to what children talk about as they incorporate the gourds into their play. When talking with children as they play with the gourds, mention their attributes *(bumpy, smooth, striped).*

7. To encourage children to notice and describe similarities and differences, make sure that your dress-up clothing fastens in different ways — with snaps, Velcro, buttons, and zippers, for example.

8. Make available computer programs that provide developmentally appropriate activities involving such classification skills as identifying attributes, matching identical items, or grouping items by their attributes. Try, for example, *Observation and Classification* (Hartley Courseware, Inc.), *East Street* (Mindplay), or *Muppetville* (Sunburst Communications, Inc.).

CLASSIFICATION

Recall Time

1. Play the "I See" game: "I see something in the art area Jason used today. It's shiny, has finger holes, and cuts paper. Can you guess what it is?" Encourage the children to give clues about something they worked with or saw another child work with.

2. Hide objects (in a bag or sock, or under a cloth) that you saw children using at work time. Encourage each child to feel an object and describe its attributes. Ask questions like "Is it hard?" "Is it squishy?" "Would it fit inside your pants pocket?" "Can you make a sound with it?"

3. As you talk with children about what they did at work time, use the terms *same* and *different:* "Danny spent all of work time in the block area. Did anyone do something *different?*" [Pause for responses.] "Yes, Vanessa, you painted with your fingers, and Elliott did the *same* thing with his fingers."

At recall time, hide objects in a bag that you saw children using at work time. Encourage children to describe the attributes of the objects they feel in the bag.

4. Occasionally, try using *not* statements at recall time: "There was one area today where teachers and children did *not* play. Do you know what area it was?"

1. Give each child a container with a variety of small objects they can sort and match, for example, styrofoam pieces, rubber bands, buttons, bottlecaps, corks, coins, paper clips. Within each collection, include several identical items, since younger children begin sorting by matching identical objects. As children work, listen to what they say and converse with them to find out what they understand about how they are sorting their items.

CLASSIFICATION

Small-Group Time

2. Bring a box of old socks for the children to play with, making sure that there are at least two to three socks per child. Encourage children to use their socks in several different ways: stretching them, fitting them on their hands, feet, and heads, turning them inside out. Talk with children about what they are doing. Encourage them to describe the attributes of their socks and to find socks that match.

A collection of old socks is the starting point for a small-group activity in which children sort and match socks and notice and describe their attributes.

3. Give each child a collection of different kinds of paper — for example, waxed paper, aluminum foil, construction paper, crepe paper, paper towels. Encourage children to examine and describe the papers' similarities and differences. Add eye droppers so children can see and describe what happens when they drop water on each sample.

4. Encourage children to examine and describe the similarities of and differences between pomegranates and apples. Make sure each child has a sample of each fruit. Listen for, and repeat the words children use to describe their fruit samples. Describe your own experiences with the fruits in a conversational manner.

5. Make jello with the children. Give each child his or her own container so each can make a separate batch. Give them extra tidbits like marshmallows, raisins, and banana slices to add to the jello, and encourage children to notice which of these additions *sink* and which *float.*

6. Bring pictures from magazines and encourage children to choose pictures they like to make collages. As children assemble their collages, encourage them to describe the attributes of the pictures they have chosen. Some older children may look for and arrange their collages by categories, for example, *things with wheels, things with noses, things we like to eat.*

7. Give each child a container with a small magnet and a set of metal and nonmetal objects: for example, pennies, paper clips, pieces of paper. Encourage children to experiment with and describe which objects are attracted to the magnet. Watch and listen closely. Some children may be able to make *not* statements: "These things stick to the magnet, but not these."

1. For an active approach to using and describing something in several different ways, give each child a small paper bag stuffed with newspaper. Make up a song about the different things you can do with it, using the children's ideas as well as your own. For example, to the tune of "Put Your Finger in the Air," sing one of these: "Throw the bag in the air." "Put the bag next to your ear." "Hide the bag under your legs."

2. Take turns having each child describe and do a nonlocomotor motion (motion in place) for the rest of the children to imitate. When everyone has had a turn, ask children to try doing two nonlocomotor motions: "Can you wiggle your fingers and move your hands up and down?" [Pause for response.] "Can you bounce your legs and pat your knees?" After giving a couple of suggestions, see if a child can combine two motions for everyone to imitate.

3. Bring toys from different work areas to the circle. Make up songs that describe their attributes. Once the children know the words, add motions to act them out. For example, to the tune of "He's Got the Whole World in His Hands," sing "The truck has four wheels that go around and around, . . . Oh yes, it does." See what motions the children can think of to add to this verse.

CLASSIFICATION

Circle Time

SERIATION

The ability to **seriate** — to order things by size, intensity, or some other dimension — is an important reasoning skill that is developing in the preschool years. Children are seriating when they can arrange a set of blocks in order from smallest to largest, when they deliberately make their voices progressively louder, or when they rank their toys from most favorite to least favorite.

The ability to seriate develops from the ability to compare, so adults should encourage preschool children to **make comparisons** frequently as well as to seriate sets of objects. Preschool children are also able, eventually, to **combine seriation and one-to-one correspondence** by ordering matched sets of objects — for example, matching the small block with the small stick, and arranging it next to the medium block with the medium stick, and next to that the large block and the large stick. Size is the obvious dimension used in many seriation activities, but don't neglect other seriation experiences using all the senses. Children enjoy ordering things by loudness, sweetness, smelliness, and wetness, for example.

The following **key experiences in seriation** provide guidelines for appropriate seriation activities.

Thin and thick paintbrushes encourage children to compare along a single dimension.

- ☐ Comparing along a single dimension: bigger/smaller/ lighter, rougher/smoother, louder/softer, harder/softer, longer/ shorter, taller/shorter, wider/narrower, etc.
- ☐ Arranging several things in order along some dimension and describing their relationships (the longest one, the shortest one, etc.)
- ☐ Fitting one ordered set of objects to another through trial and error

Planning Time

1. Having seriated sets of objects in the classroom allows you to stretch children's thinking at planning time. For example, if the child says, "I'm going to play with the teddy bear in the house area," the teacher can respond, "Are you going to use the *small, medium,* or *large* teddy bear?"

Providing sets of similar objects in graduated sizes encourages children to incorporate seriation into their play.

2. Have three different shades of blue (or any other color) paper at the planning table. Ask each child if he or she wants to make a plan on the *"light blue* paper, the *medium blue* paper, or the *dark blue* paper." Children can then draw or trace materials they will work with or dictate a plan to the teacher.

3. Have three different sizes of paper for children to choose from. After a child chooses a small, medium or large piece, ask him or her to select a thin, medium, or thick crayon to draw or trace a plan with or for the adult to use in writing down his or her dictated plan.

4. Introduce planning with a guessing game that encourages children to make a comparison: "The first person who will tell us her plan today is the girl with the *curliest* hair [the *darkest* shirt]." Repeat this process until all children have planned.

5. Ask, "Is anybody going to the *wettest* area [the water table] in our classroom today at work time?"

6. Place some objects that children have been using at work time on the table. Ask the children, "Are you going to work with something *larger* or *smaller* [heavier or lighter, thicker or thinner] than this?"

1. Add dolls and clothing in graduated sizes to the house area so that children have the opportunity to seriate as they play with the dolls — for example, by dressing the small doll in the small hat, the medium-sized doll in the medium hat, and the large doll in the large hat.

2. Collect maple (oak, eucalyptus) leaves of different sizes. Add them to the art area for collage making or to the house area for pretend food. As children incorporate them into their play, converse with them about how they are using or arranging the different-sized leaves.

3. Add objects of graduated sizes to work areas (nesting bowls, nesting boxes, nuts and bolts, measuring cups and spoons, paint swatches from the hardware store, a canister set, twigs of varying thicknesses to use as paintbrushes). As children use these seriated materials, watch and listen to see if they compare or order them.

As children play with seriated materials, watch and listen to see if they compare and order them.

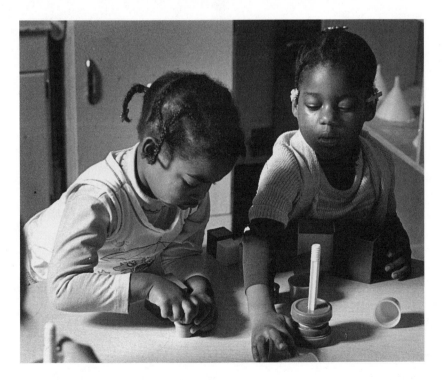

4. Go for a walk with children and collect rocks of different sizes and weights. Add them and a scale to the toy or block area so that children can experiment and talk about how rock size and weight affect the position of the scale.

5. Encourage children to extend their play by talking about seriation concepts: "Since you painted this picture with a *very thin* brush, maybe next time you'll choose a *very thick* brush."

6. Add books and/or flannel-board materials that deal with graduated sizes to the book area *(The Three Bears, The Three Billy Goats Gruff).*

7. When children have begun seriating real objects, make available appropriate computer programs, such as *Size and Logic* and *Patterns and Sequences* from Hartley Courseware, Inc., that enable them to compare the sizes of items on the computer screen and to complete partial patterns of objects. Introduce such programs first in small-group activities before offering them as a choice at work time.

SERIATION

Recall Time

1. Ask children to bring the *biggest* (or *smallest*) object they worked with to the table to talk about as they recall what they did.

2. Bring three straws to the table. Hold them in your hand so the ends look even. Let three children choose one straw each. Have the child with the longest straw recall first, the child with the second longest next, and so on. Suggested language: "The person with the *longest* straw will be the first to recall today. I see Mike and Gregory each have *long* straws. How can we tell which is *longest?*"

3. Ask three children to stand up. With the children, pick the tallest [shortest] child and ask him or her to recall first. The next tallest [shortest] goes next, and so on. Repeat this process in groups of two or three until each child has recalled.

4. When children bring materials they have used or made to recall time, look for opportunities to compare and order: "Tell us about the kinds of brushes you used, Yvonne, to make these *thick* lines and these *thin* lines."

SERIATION

Small-Group Time

1. Provide yarn and thick straws of three lengths and encourage children to string them. As they work, talk with them about the sizes of the straw pieces they are stringing.

2. Stuff different-sized paper bags with newspaper. Tape over the ends. Ask children to think up and try out different ways to use them, for example, to toss them around like balls, to paint them, or to make a "snow person." Encourage children to compare and order as they work with the bags: "Will it take *longer* to paint the *bigger* bags or the *littler* bags?" "Which bag will you put on the bottom of your snowman, the *biggest* bag or the *smallest?*"

3. Make butter with the children, encouraging children to make comparisons and to notice gradual changes. Start by giving each child a clear plastic shaker of cream. As children shake their cream containers, encourage them to observe and talk about how the cream changes from a thin liquid to a thicker solid. Encourage children to shake their containers in different ways *(faster, slower, as high as you can)*. Save some cream so that the children can compare their butter to the cream.

4. Make pancakes with the children. Make some huge ones, some very tiny ones, and some middle-sized ones. Have children choose and describe the ones they want to eat.

5. Provide each child with two sets of materials in three sizes that fit together. For example, graduated canisters and lids, or nuts and bolts in three widths. As children fit their materials together, listen to what they say about how they figured out which lid went with which canister, for example.

6. Provide a set of objects in a range of sizes (corks, cookie cutters, sponges, etc.) and print with them by dipping in paint. Encourage children to notice and label the different sizes of the prints that the corks make. Use language like *smallest, medium-size,* and *largest.*

7. Let children carve pumpkins with blunt knives and explore the contents. Encourage children to make comparisons like *scarier/not as scary, heavier/lighter, bumpier/smoother, wetter/drier.*

1. Read *Titch* by Pat Hutchinson and other stories relating to sizes.

2. Play "Red Rover, Red Rover." Build in opportunities for children to make comparisons, by saying, for example, "Let anyone shorter than Mrs. Smith come over."

Stuff paper bags of various sizes with newspapers. Encourage children to compare and order as they work with the bags.

SERIATION

Circle Time

3. Play "Simon Says," emphasizing comparisons: "Run to something that is *softer than the sidewalk/fatter than the telephone pole.*" After a few turns, see if a child can generate a similar place to run using comparison terms.

4. Play "Mother May I," giving children concrete things against which to compare when you give directions. For example, instead of saying "Take a giant step," say, "Take a step that is longer than this block."

NUMBER

Children at the preschool level are beginning to understand and use such quantitative skills as **estimating, comparing quantities and sizes, one-to-one matching, counting,** and **measuring.** Children develop an understanding of such number concepts by working with groupings of objects and solving mathematical problems that arise in their play. All of the following activities, for example, will develop an understanding of number concepts: sorting, matching, and grouping buttons of various sizes and shapes; making a garage out of blocks big enough for a toy truck; assigning a toy bear to each "bedroom" of a toy house. In contrast to these kinds of "hands-on" activities, rote drills and workbook-style exercises may enable children to memorize arithmetic facts, but may not increase their understanding of the concepts behind these facts.

Two key concepts that young children must master before they can understand formal math are **one-to-one correspondence** and **conservation of number.** When children match two sets of objects one to one — for example, when they set four places at a table with toy teacups or pass out one cookie to each child in a group — they are experiencing one-to-one correspondence. To count accurately, children must master one-to-one correspondence. Skill at rote counting doesn't necessarily mean the child can actually count — it may only indicate that he or she has memorized a sequence of number names. Though it is important for children learning to count to practice this sequence, they also need many experiences with one-to-one correspondence.

Conservation of number is the concept that the quantity of objects in a group remains the same, no matter how the objects are arranged or positioned. Preschoolers frequently make errors in estimating quantities because they haven't mastered this concept; for example, when looking at two equal piles of paper clips, one spread out on the table and the other clumped together, they will guess that the spread-out pile contains more clips because it appears larger. An understanding of conservation of number develops gradually, as children group and regroup quantities of objects and make guesses about sizes and quantities. Don't try to speed up the process by over-correcting children's mistaken estimates or by insisting on counting too early.

The following **key experiences in number** provide guideposts for activities that help develop children's understanding of number:

- ☐ Comparing number and amount: more/less, same amount
- ☐ Arranging two sets of objects in one-to-one correspondence
- ☐ Counting objects

Playing with Bristle Blocks and small bears provides natural opportunities for estimating: "There's only room for one bear in this plane."

Planning Time

1. Arrange to have more (or fewer) chairs than children at your planning table. With children, count out how many extra chairs there are or the number of additional chairs needed. When children have solved this one-to-one correspondence problem, planning begins.

2. Before planning begins, count the children at the planning table. Pose questions like this: "If Sam came to our planning table, how many people would there be?"

3. Incorporate questions about number and amount when talking to children about their plans: *"How many* blocks will your garage take, Noah?" "Will you need *a lot* of glue or *a little* glue for your cards, Renee?" *"How many* people will you work with at the hospital, Lela?"

4. Use toy telephones as a prop for planning, drawing attention to the numbers on the dial or on the push buttons: "I'm going to dial the *Number 1* and ask Zack about his plan. [Zack gives his plan.] What number should I call next?" If you have children who can interpret number symbols, give them a written "phone number" and use language like: "I'm calling *Number 6. Number 6,* what is your plan for today?"

Assign each child a phone number, and use telephones as a prop for planning: "I'm calling Number 8. Noah, can you give me your plan?"

5. Use numbers with children who are ready to make more than one plan: "Thank you for telling me your *number one* plan. Do you have a *number two* plan also?"

6. Ask children to go to the areas they will work in and bring back *two* or *three* things they plan to work with. Ask younger children to "Bring *two* things, *one for each of your hands.*"

1. As you work with children, use number language that relates to their play: "I see you made *two* pictures today, Mia. You can carry *one* in each hand when you go home today." "You still have *some* holes left to fill up in the pegboard, Frankie. Let's *count* to see *how many.*" "What a good idea you had making some of the muffins with a *few* acorns and some muffins with *lots more* acorns. I'll have the muffin that has the *most* acorns."

2. Ask the children questions that relate to number as they work: *"How many more* blocks do you think you need to finish your building, Jessica?" "You put together *two* puzzle pieces. *How many more* pieces are there for you to fit together?"

3. Add materials to the classroom for children to arrange in one-to-one correspondence: for example, equal numbers of napkins and plates, or

Matching each buttonhole with each button is a hands-on experience in one-to-one correspondence.

dolls and blankets, in the house area, lids and paint containers at the easel, hooks and smocks in the art area.

4. Make a set of number cards, each showing a large numeral and a corresponding number of large, poker-chip-size dots. Store them with poker chips in the toy area so that children can match poker chips and dots in one-to-one correspondence.

5. Add books to the book area that relate to number, for example, *One Was Johnny* by Maurice Sendak.

6. Talk about number and amount when they are appropriate within the context of children's projects:

☐ "Johnny, I see you are using the cup to fill that *large* jar with water. *How many more* cups of water do you think it will take to fill the jar? [Johnny gives his estimate.] Let's count and see."
☐ "Mary, let's count *how many* blocks you used in your tower."
☐ "I'd like to make a cake for my birthday that's just like the one you have made, Tina. I am going to use the same measuring cup as you used. *How many* cups of rice did you put into your cake pan? *How many* spoons full of water should I add to the rice?"

7. Challenge children to estimate quantities: "Do you think the sand in this bucket will all fit into that milk carton?"

8. When children have begun counting real objects aloud, encourage them to improve numeral recognition and to practice counting skills by making available developmentally appropriate computer programs such as *Number Farm* from DLM and *Counting Critters* from MECC.

Use number language that relates to what children are doing: "Russell, can you carry all five things at once?"

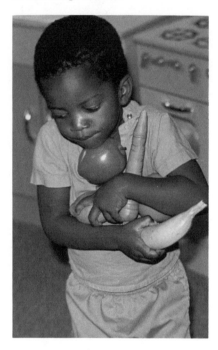

NUMBER

Recall Time

1. Give each child a bag. Ask them to put *one* thing they played with in the bag and bring it back to the table. Give each child a chance to talk about what they did with their object at work time.

2. To encourage children to count, say, "When we have *six* people at our table we will start recall."

3. Draw a picture of each interest area on a large piece of cardboard. Give each child a small pile of tokens (bears, buttons, bottlecaps). Ask them to put a token on the pictures of the area(s) they worked in. With children, count the number of tokens on each picture to see how many children worked in each area.

4. In classrooms where children use a central planning board (as described in suggestions 3–5, *Representation*), ask children to fasten the symbols for each area they worked in on the planning board next to their names or personal symbols. Refer to the board as you and the children count the number of areas children worked in: "Let's count to see how many areas Dana worked in today." "The person who worked in three areas can be the first person to recall." Compare the number of areas each child worked in.

5. Make a graph representing each area of the classroom and the number of children who worked in each area. Count the number of children who worked in each area, and encourage children to point out which areas had *a lot* of children and which areas had *a few*.

House	x x x x
Block	x x x x x x
Art	x x x x
Toy	x x x x

1. Give each child inch-cube blocks and Teddy Bear Counters and encourage them to notice number concepts as they build: "Can we make a bed *big enough* for *all three* bears?" "I see you made a long train and put a bear on each car. Can we *add* some more cars to the train for these bears?"

2. Scoop out the seeds of a pumpkin. Give each child a clump to pull apart and count.

3. Give each child a collection of small pebbles, heavy cardboard, and glue. As they make designs on their cardboard, count with children the numbers of stones they are gluing. Point out clusters of stones using number terms such as a *big* pile, a *small amount,* or a *teeny tiny* pile.

4. Ask parents to save corks. Give each child a cork and a small tin of paint. Encourage them to print dots on their paper and count them.

5. Make peanut butter-celery-raisin snacks ("ants on a log"). Ask the children how many raisins they are going to put inside the celery. Encourage them to count to verify their estimate.

6. Meet around the sand table. Provide a variety of different-sized containers and encourage children to examine and talk about number and amounts: "Do you think it will take you *more* spoonfuls of sand to fill this cup or that bowl? Let's count and see."

Circle Time

1. Read the story book *The Very Hungry Caterpillar.*

2. Let children choose a nonlocomotor motion (a movement in place such as jumping, hopping, or putting their hands up in the air, etc.) and the number of counts for which the motion should be done. Have everybody count out loud while doing the motion. When children pick huge numbers, start the counting, waiting until children raise the issue of how many that is. Then say,"That was a large number and my arms got tired, too. Let's stop at 10 this time."

3. With older children, play "One Potato, Two Potato" as a transition to the next activity.

4. Do counting songs, counting fingerplays, and counting chants with the children, for example, "Five Little Witches," "Five Little Monkeys Jumping on the Bed," "Two Little Singing Birds."

SPATIAL RELATIONS

Preschool children are beginning to become aware of **spatial relations,** a term we use to describe relationships in the physical world of objects. Spatial learning for preschoolers includes **learning things about their own bodies** — what different body parts do and how they fit together — as well as **developing their understanding of the objects around them** and the ways these objects relate to one another.

It is sometimes hard for adults to see spatial relations as an important learning area since these concepts are so much a part of everyday life that we use them automatically. Preschoolers, however, are just beginning to develop many spatial abilities that adults take for granted. They need practice, for example, in recognizing and describing the distances between and among objects, in noting the position of one object relative to another, in describing the directions things move in, and in understanding the different ways objects appear when seen from different points of view.

Remember that for a young child many simple activities pose significant **spatial problems:** for example, putting on a sweater, figuring out how big a bowl to use for a batch of green beans, rolling a ball toward a block tower and knocking it over. You can help preschoolers become more adept in spatial problem-solving by encouraging activities that include the following **key experiences in spatial relations:**

You can help children become aware of shapes by commenting on the shapes that are naturally present in the materials they choose to play with.

- ☐ Fitting things together and taking them apart
- ☐ Rearranging and reshaping objects (folding, twisting, stretching, stacking, tying)
- ☐ Observing things and places from different spatial viewpoints
- ☐ Experiencing and describing relative positions, directions, and distances
- ☐ Experiencing and representing one's own body
- ☐ Learning to locate things in the classroom, school, and neighborhood
- ☐ Interpreting representations of spatial relations in drawings and pictures
- ☐ Distinguishing and describing shapes

SPATIAL RELATIONS

Planning Time

1. Encourage children to think about and describe the relative positions of the work areas while planning. "Leah, will you work in an area that is *far away* from the planning table or *close* to it?"

2. Encourage children to observe relative positions by describing the position of the child whose turn it is to plan: "The first person to plan today is sitting *in between* Jim and Marketta." After that child has planned, ask him or her to choose and describe the position of the next person to plan. (Be aware that some children will be able to choose but unable to describe the chosen child's position.)

3. Plan with the children in an unusual place (*under* a table, *on top* of a blanket, *next* to the sink) so that they can look at the classroom from a different spatial viewpoint.

4. Make a large map of the room that shows where each of the interest areas are. Give the children a Teddy Bear Counter or a play person and ask them to walk the bear on the map from the planning table to the area in which they plan to work. As they move the bear, encourage them to describe the course he is taking — *"through* the block area, *around* the art area table. . ."

5. To help children learn to locate things in the classroom, give each child a cardboard toilet paper tube. Ask children to look through it *toward* the area they will work in and to describe the materials they will be playing with.

SPATIAL RELATIONS

Work Time

1. Add a folding vegetable steamer (or any other utensil with moving parts) to the house area and demonstrate its use to the children. Encourage children to move the pieces of the steamer around and to talk about the changes they are making as they reshape it: "Can you make the steamer *open up* like a fan?" "How far can you *close it up* until it won't close any more?" "What goes *through* the holes to cook the vegetables?"

2. Encourage children to distinguish and describe shapes by changing the shapes of the paper you use for drawing and painting. Include ovals, rectangles, squares, triangles, diamonds, etc.

3. When children are building with blocks or table toys, encourage them to look at their structures from different spatial viewpoints: "You put a cow behind your barn, Nancy. Come and see what the barn looks like to the cow."

4. Since drawing encourages children to represent spatial relations, encourage children to represent their work in pictures. "Can we draw a picture of this boat you and Elliott built, since we'll have to take it apart at clean-up time?" If the children need help getting started, point out one or two spatial positions for the children to focus on: "Let's see, the blocks go *around in a circle.* The children are *inside* the circle. Elliott, can you help draw the blocks? Jason, can you draw the people?" Hang the finished picture at the children's eye level in the same area where the work was done.

5. To encourage children to fit things together and take them apart and to rearrange and reshape materials, add geoboards with rubber bands and yarn to the toy area. (Note: geoboards are flat pieces of wood covered with nails or raised knobs on which designs can be woven with yarn, rubber bands, string, etc.).

Fitting things together and taking them apart helps children learn how the pieces of an object relate to each another.

6. Take photographs of the children in different spatial positions during outside play (hanging *upside down, at the top of* the climbing structure, etc.). Make a book out of the pictures and add it to the book area to give children opportunities to interpret spatial relations in photographs and to see their own experiences from a different spatial viewpoint.

7. To help children distinguish and describe shapes, cut shape stencils out of heavy cardboard. Put them in the art area for children to trace or paint over.

8. Make available developmentally appropriate computer programs that exercise spatial reasoning skills, such as *Stickybear Town Builder* from Weekly Reader Software. Using this program, young children create a town map and then practice their direction skills by guiding a "car" to specific destinations. Before making the program available at work time, introduce it to children in a small-group activity.

SPATIAL RELATIONS
Recall Time

1. Bring a small car to the recall table. Push the car to the child who will recall first. To give children the opportunity to describe relative directions, say something like this: "I'm pushing the car *away from* myself *toward* Joshua." After Joshua is finished recalling, ask him to describe where he will push the car next. Repeat the same process until recall is over.

2. To encourage children to observe the relative positions of the work areas, ask them to identify the area *farthest* from the recall table. Then ask who, if anyone, worked in that area. Continue this strategy with the rest of the interest areas, using words like the *next farthest* area and *closest* area.

3. Recall with your group *inside* a block structure someone made at work time so that children can see both the block structure and the classroom from a different spatial viewpoint.

SPATIAL RELATIONS
Small-Group Time

1. To encourage children to rearrange and reshape materials, ask them to create designs with paper scraps and staplers. If you do not have enough staplers for each child to have one, bring tape or paste to eliminate waiting for turns. As children work, describe spatial positions and encourage children to describe them: "Louie, your design is getting *longer.*" "I see you put three pieces of paper *on top of* the blue piece, Uri."

2. Give each child a collection of twist ties, pipecleaners, and/or rubber bands to rearrange and reshape. Describe what they are doing with the materials and model new ways to use them: "Look what happened to my pipecleaner when I *twisted* it *around* my wrist."

3. Bring large pieces of paper for each child. Encourage children to reshape their paper: "Let's see how many different ways we can think of to fold this paper."

4. Cut sponges into different shapes. Encourage children to dip them into paint and print with them.

5. Give children paper and crayons or markers so that they can trace around different parts of their bodies. Demonstrate first with one child's hand or foot. Converse with children about what they are doing and discovering.

6. Have children spread peanut butter on foods of different shapes — crackers, breads, celery, etc. Encourage children to notice and describe the different shapes they are working with.

7. To encourage folding and reshaping, have children wrap up boxes. Provide a variety of materials: several rolls of clear tape or masking tape, boxes of different sizes and shapes, scissors, all kinds and sizes of paper. Observe and support children as they attempt to solve the "fit" problems they encounter.

This child is becoming aware of spatial transformations as she folds, stretches, shapes and reshapes silly putty.

Circle Time

1. Give each child a piece of string or rope. Encourage them to experience a variety of spatial positions relative to their ropes: "Stand *on* your string and jump *up* and *down.*" "Put the rope *in between* your legs." Have children take turns thinking of and describing other ways the group can move with the ropes.

2. Give each child a small object, such as a block or poker chip. Make up a song to the tune of "Put Your Finger in the Air" ("Put the inch cube on your shoulder, on your shoulder . . ."), and have the children act it out. To help children think of their own nonlocomotor motions, ask questions like "If you wanted to put the poker chip somewhere where no one could see it, where would you put it?"

3. Play old favorite circle games like "Looby Loo," "Hokey Pokey," and "Simon Says" that encourage children to notice the positions of parts of their bodies. To ensure success, eliminate words like *left* and *right* and the trick in "Simon Says." Include children in the decision-making as you play these games. For example, when doing Hokey Pokey, after the verse that starts, "Put your foot in, Put your foot out," ask children "What should we put in next?"

Dancing to music around some hoops is one way to become aware of the concepts of *around* and *inside*.

TIME

Caring for house plants offers opportunities to observe changes over time and to anticipate the future.

The limitations of preschoolers in understanding **temporal relations** (time) are well known to any adult who has ever attempted to get a young child to a scheduled appointment. While the adult's day is divided into minutes and hours, most preschoolers do not understand precise time intervals. For the young child, time is a continuum loosely organized in **before/after** sequences, in which an awareness of the present often crowds out any thoughts of the past and the future.

Adults can help preschoolers mature in their understanding of time, not by emphasizing formal time intervals, but by focusing on the **sequence of past, present, and future.** Encourage children to think about what they have done in the past and what they plan to do in the future, and help them recognize the order in which events occur. Ask them to think about and talk about how long it will take to do things. Introduce conventional time units only when children are ready, and keep them simple: use terms like **morning, yesterday,** and **hour** in contexts that they understand. Eventually, you'll want to help children recognize what clocks and calendars are used for, but don't overemphasize them.

Keep the following **key experiences in temporal relations** in mind as you plan your day:

Understanding Time Units or Intervals

- ☐ Stopping and starting an action on signal
- ☐ Experiencing and describing different rates of speed
- ☐ Experiencing and comparing time intervals
- ☐ Observing seasonal changes
- ☐ Observing that clocks and calendars are used to mark the passage of time

Sequencing Events in Time

- ☐ Anticipating future events verbally and making appropriate preparations
- ☐ Planning and completing what one has planned
- ☐ Describing and representing past events
- ☐ Using conventional time units in talking about past and future events
- ☐ Noticing, describing, and representing the order of events

TIME

Planning Time

1. Refer to the day of the week when you begin planning: "Happy *Monday morning.*"

2. When talking to children about their plans, encourage them to think about the length of time activities will take and the sequences of events: "How *long* do you think it will take you to paint at the easel? Will you have *time* to do something else?" "What are you going to do *first, next,* and *last?*"

3. Record children's plans on a tape recorder to help them anticipate future events. Play the tape back at recall time to help children describe and represent past events.

4. This strategy is for groups who plan with a central planning board (see planning suggestions 3 – 5, *Representation*). If children choose more than one picture of materials they plan to work with, have them place the pictures on the board in sequence to represent what they will do *first, next,* and *last.*

5. For children who are developmentally ready, start planning books in which they can store their planning forms as they accumulate over time (see planning suggestions 6 and 7, *Representation*). Occasionally you may suggest that the child look through his or her planning book prior to making the day's plan. If children enjoy writing, you can encourage them to add the days of the week at the top of each page.

TIME

Work Time

1. Add seasonal clothing to the house area — sweaters in fall, hats and mittens in winter, umbrellas in the rainy season.

2. Place seasonal objects on a discovery table (leaves, acorns, pine cones, snow, corn, dirt) or fill the sand table with a quantity of one of these materials.

3. Put thin and thick paint in the art area. As children paint, talk with them about which one takes *longer* to dry.

4. Use the language of time in your normal conversations with children at play. For example, if children are pretending to be restaurant workers you might say, "I'm in a *big hurry today.* What's the *quickest* thing you can make me to eat?"

5. Grow mung bean and alfalfa sprouts in your science area. Encourage children to check, discuss, and represent their growth each day. Serve them on cheese sandwiches for a healthy snack and encourage children to recall how long it took to grow them.

	Juice	Napkins	Cups	Snack Basket
Monday				
Tuesday	◇	✚	☆	⌐
Wednesday	☆			◁
Thursday				
Friday				

A simple picture calendar of the week helps children recognize whose turn it is to pour juice, pass out napkins, pass out cups, or pass the snack basket.

6. Put a modified clock showing the daily routine next to the traditional clock. Divide the clock like a pie chart with segments to represent each part of the daily routine. Be sure that the segments are proportional to the amount of time the parts of the routine actually take. For example, work time should be a larger piece of the pie than planning time. Label each segment with pictures as well as words. Keep this special clock at the child's eye level.

7. To encourage children to practice stopping and starting, tape a red symbol to the stop button and a green symbol to the start button of the classroom tape recorder.

8. Add sand timers to the classroom work areas. As children work with materials, encourage them to anticipate how long an activity will take: "Do you think you'll be able to *finish* stringing your necklace *before* the sand in the sand timer gets to the bottom?"

9. To help children anticipate future events, make a weekly calendar showing whose turn it is to feed the animals, water the plants, and signal for clean-up time. The chart can include words for the days of the week, the children's symbols and names, and small pictures that represent each task. *(See photo.)*

10. Add containers to your sand area that have different-sized holes in them so that children can experience and describe different rates

A sand timer made from plastic bottles is a concrete tool that helps children become aware of the length of time intervals.

Remembering to put on her snow pants before her boots is a valuable sequencing experience for this child.

of speed. Encourage children to talk about how the sand moves more *quickly* or more *slowly* through the different-sized holes: "Boy, it takes a *long time* for the sand to go through that little hole. Let's see if it will go any faster through a great big hole."

11. To encourage children to use conventional time units connected with age, ask parents to bring in family photos that show family members of different ages. Encourage children to talk about the *youngest,* and *oldest* member of their families.

12. To encourage children to observe seasonal changes, add budding forsythia branches and pussywillows to your house area in the spring so that children can watch and talk about the buds as they change to flowers and pussywillows.

13. Make a simplified weekly or monthly calendar to put in the house area. In addition to using numerals, represent each day through pictures and symbols that have concrete meanings for preschoolers. For example, find pictorial ways to represent school days versus stay-at-home days, birthdays, special field trips, and holidays. If you don't know what picture to use for a particular event, ask the children for their ideas.

14. After any holiday, special occasion, or field trip, provide materials that will invite children to describe and represent the event after it has past. For example, in November, make sure there are costume-making materials in the art area so children can represent their Halloween experiences. You may also add a box of donated costumes to the house area.

15. Once children have had a variety of classroom experiences with starting and stopping an action on signal, make available the computer activity "Choo Choo" from Lawrence Hall of Science's *Estimation* program.

TIME

Recall Time

1. Play back the tape recording you made of children planning. As you listen with children, listen to their spontaneous comments and when possible, encourage children to notice and compare time periods. "Zachary, you said your plan would take *a little while* to finish. Was that true?" "Julie did you work on your painting for *all* of work time?"

2. To encourage children to describe past events, use the tune of "Are You Sleeping," making up songs with the children about what they did at work time: "What did you do, Zack? What did you do, Zack? At work time, at work time? Tell us what you did today, Tell us what you did today. At work time, at work time." "Zack built a tower, Zack built a tower. At work time. . . ."

3. After returning from a field trip, ask children to draw pictures of what they remember. If possible, take "instant" photos during the trip to use in the recall process. Collect the photos in a booklet and add it to your book area so that children can "relive" their field trip experiences whenever they want.

TIME

Small-Group Time

1. During each season, have children collect natural materials and make seasonal collages. Display them at children's eye level so that throughout the year you can refer to them to encourage children to recall past seasons and discuss the present season.

2. Adopt a neighborhood tree. Walk the children to the tree several times a year, take photographs of it, and take dictation from the children about the changes they notice. Make a book from the photos and the children's dictated observations and add it to the book area.

3. To help children anticipate future events and recall past events, plant bulbs in the fall with the children. Take photos of the bulbs and the children planting them so that children can look at them in the spring when the flowers appear.

4. Place a large sheet of paper on the floor and pass out crayons for drawing on it. Play some slow music and then some fast music. As the children color to the music, note whether children color quickly or slowly to match the rate of speed of the music. Talk with them to find out how they experienced the different musical tempos.

5. Bury an old and a new sock in the ground. Dig them up several times a month and encourage the children to talk about the changes they notice.

6. On the day before a classroom party, give children materials to make placemats to help them anticipate and prepare for the party.

7. Expose children to cooking and mixing activities that involve sequences of events; for example, making sandwiches, mixing ingredients for play dough, making paints for the art area. Upon completing each recipe or process, encourage the children to recall the sequence in which they added ingredients. "What did you put in your bowl first, Justin?"

TIME

Circle Time

Pouring juice offers practice in starting and stopping an action on signal.

1. To help children anticipate future events, read storybooks with repetitive refrains *(The Gingerbread Boy, The Fly Went By, Ask Mr. Bear, Journey Cake, Ho)*. Once the children are familiar with the story and its refrain, pause before the refrain to encourage the children to repeat it on their own.

2. For the experience of stopping and starting on signal, play musical chairs, allowing children to select the type of locomotor motion (movement from place to place) they will use to travel around the chairs (jumping, taking baby steps, etc.). Make sure there are always enough chairs for all the children. Do not take away chairs after each turn because this leaves many of the children waiting and watching and often creates management problems. Having all the children participate in each round keeps the focus on starting and stopping an action on signal.

3. Using paper plates that children have decorated with streamers, ask children to pat different parts of their bodies when the music starts and to stop patting when the music stops. Before you start the music again each time, have children choose a different part of their bodies to pat.

4. With older children, play "Red Light, Green Light." Encourage children to take turns being the leader who gives the stop and go signals.

5. To help children recall past events and temporal sequences, make up songs about a cooking activity the children have just experienced at small-group time. Use the children's words. For example, to the tune of "She'll Be Comin' 'Round the Mountain," sing: "First we cracked the peanuts, yes we did, yes we did. First we cracked the peanuts, yes we did, yes we did. . . ." Additional verses might begin: "Then we threw them in the blender," "Then we pushed the blender button," "It made a loud sound," and so on.

6. Make a paper chain to help children mark the passage of time. Start with five links on the chain to mark the passage of a school week. To signal the end of the day, choose one child to cut off a link. Later you can make longer chains to represent longer time periods, for example, the number of school days before Halloween. For another variation on this very simple "count-down" calendar, place five (or whatever number of days is appropriate) rocks in a clear plastic jar. Remove one rock at the end of each day. Or, blow up five balloons and pop one at the end of each day.

Date: April 5, 1988

Key Experience Focus: Spatial relations

Theme: Springtime

Plans	Reactions to the Day

Plans

Planning Time

Ruth's table — Bring a blanket to the planning table and make a tent with it to gather *under.* Be sure that one end of the tent is still open so that children can see the interest areas as they plan.

Ann's table — Ask Clara, Ben, and Nicole to go to the interest areas, find the materials they will use at work time, and bring them back to the planning table. While they are hunting their items, plan with Jason, Suzanne, and Angela using a paper towel tube. Ask one child at a time to look *through* the tube *towards* the area they plan to work in. Ask the other children to guess what the child who is planning is looking at. If children are curious about Ruth's group planning under the table, suggest that your group do recall time that way.

Work Time

1. Cut easel paper into various shapes (diamonds, squares, rectangles, ovals). Use shape terms when talking to children: "I see you chose a *diamond-shaped* paper to draw a picture on. It has four straight edges." "*Which shape* will you use to paint your picture?"

Reactions to the Day

Planning Time

All three planning strategies were successful, but I'd make one change in the paper towel tube strategy. Next time, I'd give each child his or her own tube, so that when the child who is planning is looking towards an area, all the children can try to spot the materials and toys that child will work with.

Work Time

The most fascinating part of putting the different shapes of easel paper in the art area was watching the children solve the problem of how to hang them up. Ben noticed that the diamond-shaped paper "could only fit one clothespin at the top." Clara said, "Look, there's one paper that looks like my sign." She wanted to paint on it, but the sides kept folding up and she needed help seeing that the clothespins could be attached to the sides of the easel as well as to the top.

Work Time, continued

The following is intended to represent the ideas generated during the entire *planning process for one day's activities, including ideas raised in team discussions (but not necessary recorded in written form) and the thought processes of the team members as they reflect upon the day. The actual written plan and reactions would be much briefer.*

Plans	**Reactions to the Day**

(Work Time, continued)

2. Take sand out of the sand table and fill the table with dirt and gardening items (several pairs of gardening gloves, trowels, planting containers, empty seed packets).

3. Put magnifying glasses and the materials needed for planting grass seed in the science area.

4. Encourage children to look at the work they are doing from different spatial viewpoints. Use the words *back, front, other side,* and *upside down.* Note whether or not each child can respond appropriately.

5. Add forsythia and pussywillow branches to the house area. Put some in water and leave some dry so you can compare what happens to them.

Recall Time

Ruth's table — Bring a ball of string to the table. Hold the end of the string and ask a child to unroll the ball until she gets to the area and toy she played with at work time. (While the other children are waiting, encourage them to talk about where the string is going.) When the child reaches the area she worked in, ask her to talk about what she did. Cut off the string, and after three children have taken their turns, compare the lengths of the strings and the distances they represent: "Let's see who has the shortest string and worked in the area closest to our table."

Ann's table — Have the group recall under the table. Send two children out at a time, asking each to get a toy they worked with. While the others are waiting, talk about what they can see from under the table, and have them guess which child is coming back by looking at their feet and legs only.

Children needed more time just to explore the dirt in the sand table before they were ready to work with the grass seed in the science area. The concept of putting seed inside a cup, filling it over with dirt, and leaving it there was not as appealing as simply playing with the dirt.

Jason made a crayon picture of a person. Ruth held it up and talked about the front of the picture, then turned it over and said, "Oh, I see you only drew the front and not the back." They talked about the different things you would see on the front and the back of a person — he focused primarily on the lack of a face and the long hair. Then he flipped the paper over and drew the person's back.

Recall Time

The ball of string recall strategy was confusing for children. While children understood the idea of unrolling the ball until they reached the area they played in, they were not able to understand the comparison between the lengths of string. Though they realized that some children's strings were long and others short, they did not understand the relationship between the lengths of the string and the distance traveled. I would like to repeat this activity again in three months to see if the children are able to understand it better.

Plans	**Reactions to the Day**

Small-Group Time

Ann's table — Have children make designs with paper scraps and staplers. Before passing out staplers, ask a couple of the children to help you demonstrate how they work. Use spatial language: "First you slide the paper *in between* these two parts, then you press it *down* hard until you hear it click."

Ruth's table — Do paint printing with sponges cut into shapes of various sizes. Involve children in the preparation work, stressing spatial terms. When children are putting on the smocks, use their shape symbols instead of their names, for example asking "Triangle" to help "Circle" out with the Velcro on her smock. Ask for help *spreading* the newspaper out until it *covers the whole table.* Use paint containers of different sizes and shapes. As children paint, make observations about which sponges *fit inside* which paint containers.

Circle Time

Play music and ask children to move until they hear the music stop, then freeze in their positions. While they are "frozen," ask children to describe the positions of their bodies. If they don't have the language yet, provide it for them: "I see you have one leg out *sideways* from your body and an arm *reaching up high* to the sky." "You are lying flat on the ground with your eyes looking *up towards* the ceiling."

Small-Group Time

Ben spent all of small-group time working to get a staple in his paper scrap. Angela stapled one big piece of paper in the middle and then stapled lots of little pieces of paper at each end. She told me it was "ants carrying away a sandwich at a picnic."

Most children used the sponge shapes to paint on their hands, instead of paper, except for Ivan, who cried and said he didn't want to get his hands dirty. I suggested he hold the sponge with a clothespin when he dipped it in the paint. I must remember this about him when we do messy activities in the future.

Circle Time

The adults ended up doing most of the describing for the children. We'll repeat this activity tomorrow to see if any of the children are able to describe their body positions when the newness of the activity has worn off.

Sample Child Assessment Record (CAR)

Child's Name: Catie L.

Remember to date all entries.

Active Learning

9/28
Did the actions to the song, "Open, Shut Them."

10/20
Guessed we were having peanut butter at snack by smelling.

12/1
When asked to show us a way to get to the planning tables, hopped on one foot.

12/6
When tape got tangled in dispenser, used scissors to cut it off.

12/9
Moved sideways the entire length of the railroad ties at outside time.

Language

9/7
Pointed to the art area during planning time and said, "I want to go there."

9/20
When asked who she would like to sit next to at circle, she said, "Amber, Pamber."

10/4
After the story "Good Night Moon," she said, "Good night fire."

Representation

9/9
Used scissors to cut up play dough. Called them french fries.

10/7
Moved metal cars while making motor sounds.

10/10
Used the Bristle Blocks to make a camera. Asked others to say "cheese."

11/11
Asked if she could be the mom in block area play.

Classification

9/30
Built four separate structures with the inch cubes, each a single color. All were different colors.

11/19
Sorted the corks from the buttons at clean-up time.

11/21
Separated the shiny stones from the dull ones at outside time. Labeled the shiny ones "Diamonds in my hands."

11/30
Said the puppet was made with modeling clay, not play dough.

Seriation

10/17
Turned the nesting cups upside down and stacked them from largest to smallest.

10/27
Told me her bag would be "too heavy" if she collected another rock.

Number

9/27
Said, "I need more colors on my picture."

9/21
Counted out 10 napkins for the snack basket.

11/4
After building a spaceship with blocks, said, "21, 18, 12, blast off."

Space

9/12
At clean-up time, when asked to put the paint brushes inside the pitcher, was able to do this.

10/14
Made a "bed" using four large wooden blocks to make a rectangle on the floor. Brought two pillows from the toy area and a blanket from the block area. Got inside the structure and covered up.

11/18
Played with the silly putty by letting it flow from the table top into a container she held on the floor.

Time

9/16
At planning time, said she wanted to make a bed again.

11/12
When finished with snack, put cup in sink and napkin in trash and found a place at the circle without being told it was circle time.

11/16
Reminded us that it was getting close to clean-up time.

Sources of Songs and Fingerplays

The following collections contain many songs and fingerplays that can be used with the activities and strategies suggested in the text.

Beall, Pamela Conn and Susan Hagen Nipp. *Wee Sing Around the Campfire.* Los Angeles: Price/Stern/Sloan Publishers, Inc., 1982.

_____. *Wee Sing Children's Songs and Fingerplays.* Los Angeles: Price/Stern/Sloan Publishers, Inc., 1982.

_____. *Wee Sing Silly Songs.* Los Angeles: Price/Stern/Sloan Publishers, Inc., 1982.

Dallin, Leon and Lynn Dallin. *Heritage Songster: 320 Folk and Familiar Songs.* Dubuque, Iowa: William C. Brown Company Publishers, 1966.

Glazer, Tom. *Eye Winker, Tom Tinker, Chin Chopper: Fifty Musical Fingerplays.* Garden City, New York: Doubleday & Company, Inc., 1973.

Haines, B. Joan E., and Linda L. Gerber. *Leading Young Children to Music: A Resource Book for Teachers.* Columbus, Ohio: Charles E. Merrill Publishing Co., 1980.

Weikart, Phyllis S. *Movement Plus Rhymes, Songs, & Singing Games: Activities for Children Ages 3 to 7.* Ypsilanti, Michigan: High/Scope Press, 1988.

Winn, Marie, ed. *The Fireside Book of Children's Songs.* New York: Simon and Schuster, 1966.

Wirth, Marian, et al. *Musical Games, Fingerplays and Rhythmic Activities for Early Childhood.* West Nyack, New York: Parker Publishing Co., Inc., 1983.

Michelle Graves, a senior consultant at High/Scope Educational Research Foundation, designs and conducts training workshops and long-term training projects for teachers, teacher-trainers, and educational administrators. She has also produced and written the scripts for a series of videotapes on the High/Scope Curriculum. In her training and consulting experiences, Ms. Graves has worked with a wide range of educators in Head Start and other preschool programs, in day care programs, in early elementary public school programs, and in special education settings. She also has extensive early childhood teaching experience, both in programs serving the normal range of young children and in special education settings. ∎